Racism and Justice

Also by Gertrude Ezorsky:
Philosophical Perspectives on Punishment, editor
Moral Rights in the Workplace, editor

Racism and Justice

The Case for Affirmative Action

Gertrude Ezorsky

Cornell University Press

Ithaca and London

Copyright © 1991 by Cornell University

All rights reserved. Except for brief quotations in a review, this book, or parts thereof, must not be reproduced in any form without permission in writing from the publisher. For information, address Cornell University Press, 124 Roberts Place, Ithaca, New York 14850.

First published 1991 by Cornell University Press.

International Standard Book Number 0-8014-2622-7 (cloth)
International Standard Book Number 0-8014-9922-4 (paper)
Library of Congress Catalog Card Number 91-55062

Printed in the United States of America

Librarians: Library of Congress cataloging information appears on the last page of the book.

♾ The paper in this book meets the minimum requirements of the American National Standard for Information Sciences —Permanence of Paper for Printed Library Materials, ANSI Z39.48-1984.

For my students at the City University of New York

Contents

Contents

Contents

Racism and Justice

Introduction

The affirmative action programs begun in the 1960s have been diminished in the 1980s in response to a different political climate. In this book I hope to make alive, once again, the rationales for those programs and to answer their critics.

This book focuses on black persons as beneficiaries of affirmative action in employment. In adopting that focus I do not mean to deny the entitlement of other minorities, women, or groups such as the handicapped to such benefits. Blacks, however, as descendants of slaves brought to this country against their will and as victims of the post-Reconstruction century of murderous racism, which was encouraged, practiced, and given legal sanction by our government, have a unique entitlement to special efforts to ensure their fair share of employment benefits.

An important purpose of affirmative action programs in employment may best be understood as racial desegregation of the American workplace, but the programs also significantly affect the working lives of millions of Americans—their access to professional and skill training, their place in the hierarchy of employment, and, consequently, the living standard they and their families enjoy. In this book, I argue that affirmative action is warranted on both practical and moral grounds. To understand the rationale for affirmative action, however, we must start by distancing ourselves from the controversy over its merits. Part

Introduction

I begins with an analysis of racism itself, distinguishing two forms—overt and institutional—and goes on to explicate the remedies for each. Part II offers two kinds of assessments of such remedies: the first appraises their effectiveness as instruments for ending racism; the second addresses the ethical criticisms raised by their implementation. Part III contains documents important in the development of affirmative action.

While most persons conceive racism as exemplified in racially biased actions—overt racism—the primary importance of affirmative action lies in its effectiveness as a remedy for institutional racism, by which race-neutral policies and practices can lead to the exclusion of blacks. In employment, institutional racism can occur when employees are selected through personal connections or by qualifying for certain requirements or seniority standards. These procedures are intrinsically free of race prejudice, and they exist in areas where no blacks reside. Nevertheless, these institutional procedures perpetuate the effects of overt racism. For example, unions negotiated seniority systems not to injure blacks but to give their members job security. Yet, as "last hired, first fired," blacks have been injured by seniority-based layoff and promotion. Affirmative action programs were created in large part to reduce the negative impact of institutional racism on black persons.

Programs aimed to lessen the negative impact of qualification requirements on blacks help to remedy the injury wrought by their (continuing) history as victims of racism—especially their history of segregation. For example, inferior, underfunded schools in black neighborhoods tend to render blacks vulnerable to employer tests. To reduce such vulnerability, the Supreme Court endorsed an eminently reasonable affirmative action strategy in *Griggs* v. *Duke Power Co.* (1971): if a qualification requirement has adverse impact on blacks, the employer must show that the requirement is a business necessity. *Griggs* is of historic importance because it recognizes the harm wrought by institutional racism on black persons.

Numerical goals for hiring and promoting minorities which permit preference to "basically qualified" blacks also reduce the negative effect of competence requirements. Such preference is a particularly controversial form of affirmative action because it permits exclusion of a more qualified white candidate. I suggest that while such preference is justified, some criticism of it should be taken seriously, for where white candidates are excluded in favor of less qualified (or less senior) blacks, the whites are singled out to pay a debt presumably owed by society as a whole. In my view, this effect does not mean that racial preference should be abandoned but rather that measures should be created to reduce the price of such preference for white candidates and to spread the burden of payment as widely as possible. Such measures are spelled out in Part II.

Such programs as work-sharing and giving preference to less senior blacks either for retention during layoff or for advancement tend to reduce the racially adverse effect of seniority-based selection. Some affirmative action measures, such as the advertising of positions, are beneficial not only to blacks but to white candidates who are outside the word-of-mouth network for information about job openings.

Black business entrepreneurs, like blacks in the labor market, have suffered pervasive discrimination. For example, they have been denied their fair share of government contracts. "Set-asides"—allocations of a fixed proportion of such contracts to minority enterprises—were devised as a remedy for such past discrimination and upheld in *Fullilove* v. *Klutznick* in 1980 (but invalidated in 1989).

In Part II, I answer those who have criticized affirmative action on instrumental and moral grounds. I appraise affirmative action as a practical instrument for ending racism in Chapter 3. Some critics have questioned the statistical aim of the programs; other critics suggest that the programs have increased rather than decreased racial prejudice. In assessing the general efficacy of AA programs, I show that where affirmative action requirements have been enforced they have yielded significant benefits for black people. Contrary to widespread belief, among such beneficiaries are low-status blacks who as a result of affirmative action programs were able to enter professional schools and move up in private and public employment. In this chapter, I criticize the views of such analysts as sociologist William J. Wilson who see affirmative action as largely irrelevant to the needs of truly disadvantaged blacks.

A different kind of practical criticism is offered by those who claim that affirmative action is unnecessary because other groups who also have suffered from discrimination—such as European immigrants, Asians, and West Indians—have advanced in American society without the special dispensations of affirmative action programs. I argue that such critics tend to ignore relevant factors, such as the radically different history of American blacks.

The ethical issues raised by affirmative action policy are analyzed in Chapter 4. I first address the moral justification for affirmative action programs and then turn to the moral criticisms of these programs. Ethically, the benefits of affirmative action are doubly justified. I argue that they constitute deserved compensation for past injustice: the legacy of racism, from which, according to Justice Thurgood Marshall—who rose to wear the robe of a Supreme Court justice—no black person has escaped. Affirmative action also has a forward-looking justification: it contributes to the creation of a racially impartial society, in which separation by race will have largely disappeared. We have seen not only racial separation in personal facilities, swimming pools, and the like (now contrary to law), but also occupational segregation of blacks into the lowest jobs, "hot, heavy, and dirty"—those which in large part are still performed by the descendants of slaves.

Introduction

In the latter part of Chapter 4, I take up the claims of those who see affirmative action programs as benefiting mostly affluent blacks, as restricting the right of employers, or as penalizing qualified whites. I refute these claims or suggest compensation for whites where I find them valid. Some critics also object to affirmative action programs on the ethical ground that they undermine the meritocratic principle of justice which governs American employment. As we shall see, these analysts misconstrue the actuality of our world of work.

Throughout this book I frequently rely on investigations carried out by social scientists—sociologists, historians, and economists—because, in my view, moral philosophers' analyses of public policy issues should be relevant to social reality. Social science investigations serve as a check on a biased perception of that reality from which none of us is free.

Over the years, critical investigations and court opinions have led to or enforced affirmative action policies, and I present excerpts from a few of them in Part III. A 1972 Equal Employment Opportunity Commission study details the impact of overt and institutional racism in the Bell Telephone System. *Griggs* v. *Duke Power Co.* (1971; now weakened) requires that employers prove that their qualification tests that disproportionately exclude minorities serve a business necessity. *United Steelworkers* v. *Weber* (1979) required an employer to reserve a certain number of places for blacks for training opportunities. In a 1980 report, Eleanor Holmes Norton, former chair of the EEOC, recommends work-sharing as an antidote for laying off blacks. A court order (subsequently withdrawn) which resulted from *Vulcan Pioneers* v. *New Jersey Department of Civil Service* (1984) gave blacks preferential treatment in municipal layoffs, but the judge ordered federal compensation for whites who would otherwise have kept their jobs. When, contrary to an earlier decision, government set-asides of contracts for minority companies were denied by the Supreme Court in 1989, Justice Marshall (joined by two other justices) dissented; his opinion appears in *City of Richmond* v. *J. A. Croson Co.* Finally, I offer Supreme Court Justice Marshall's eloquent argument for the historical justification of affirmative action, which appears in the opinion he wrote in 1978 (partly concurring with the majority opinion, partly dissenting) for *Regents of University of California* v. *Bakke.*

These materials are the underpinnings for a rationale of affirmative action, and I write this book in the hope that despite the recent weakening of affirmative action they will not be forgotten.

Part I

Racism and Its Remedies

I

Overt and Institutional Racism

Overt racist action, as conceived here, takes place only if a harm is inflicted or a benefit withheld either because of the perpetrator's racial bias against the victim or because of that perpetrator's obliging the race prejudice of others.[1] (Thus an employer who refuses to hire blacks because of concern for white customers' or white employees' bias is practicing overt racism.) Racially biased persons are disposed to treat blacks in an irrational and negative manner because of their race. The victim of overt racism may be a black group as well as an individual, such as residents of a segregated school district, which because of overt racism is denied equal funding.

How does institutional racism differ from the overt type?

Institutional racism occurs when a firm uses a practice that is race-neutral (intrinsically free of racial bias) but that nevertheless has an adverse impact on blacks as a group. For example, to obtain a position, a worker often needs specific training or skilled work experience. If blacks tend to lack such qualifications, they

1. Some points in this book draw on material used in my article "Discrimination," forthcoming in the *Encyclopedia of Ethics* (New York: Garland).

9

are excluded disproportionately from employment. Yet job qualification standards are intrinsically free of bias: not only are they used in all-white areas; they would most likely exist in a racially impartial society.

But while competence criteria are inherently bias-free, their negative impact on blacks perpetuates the effects of overt racism. For example, as a result of overtly racist "last-hired, first fired" policies toward blacks and the favoring of whites for on-the-job training, many blacks have been unable to gain work experience, particularly special working skills. Two other widely used hiring practices, selection by personal connections and selection by seniority ranking—also in themselves bias free—tend to bar blacks from desirable positions.

The adverse effect on blacks of these neutral practices also contributes to the perpetuation of racist attitudes. Individuals growing up in a society where blacks are visibly predominant in the lowest jobs tend to believe that blacks naturally belong there.

When the adverse impact of bias-free practices occurs in a society where, generally speaking, such impact is in significant part either a result of overt racism, or a contribution to its perpetuation, then that impact is appropriately called *racist impact*. Such impact is characteristic of institutional racism. It is important to remember that those who administer procedures having racist impact may not themselves be racist, that is, they may not personally have racist attitudes.

I have attempted to distinguish the concepts of overt and institutional racism, but in reality they often work together. For example, although qualification requirements are in themselves race-neutral, biased employers or union officials can manipulate them to exclude blacks. Such manipulation was common in the post–1964 Civil Rights Act period, when, as we shall see, employers and some unions fearful of an influx of blacks raised qualification standards in order to keep them out.

Overt Racism

Statistics showing that blacks disproportionately occupy low-paying, undesirable jobs conflate the disproportionate effects of both types of racism.

Some methods for detecting overt racism in hiring practices are more effective than others. For example, some sociologists estimate employer racial discrimination by determining whether blacks and whites with equal productive characteristics—for example, education and work experience—receive equal payoffs in employment. Unequal payoffs not explained by unequal productive characteristics define the measure of employment "discrimination."

This method is irrelevant to my analysis, however, because it fails to distinguish the effect of overt employer racism from the powerful racist impact of a significant racially neutral practice—selection by personal connections. The advantage of this widespread recruitment method to whites is very great, for their employed white friends and relatives lead them to remunerative positions. Because of such connections, whites who are no more productive than blacks will tend to receive a better payoff. Recruitment by personal connections, however, does not necessarily reflect overt employer racism. A firm may rely on recruitment by personal contacts because they save job advertising costs or because the employer believes that such referrals are reliable, or because employees are quick to spot opportunities for friends. A better method for assessing overt racism in hiring is the systematic use of "testers," whereby black and white applicants apply for a specific position. The selection can determine whether they are impartially treated by employers. However, no such direct testing has been extensively carried out during the past decade. [But see the Postscript, p. 27, below.]

Nevertheless, overt racism in employment practices can be

assessed indirectly, through extrapolation. If overtly racist behavior, as well as racist attitudes—that is, dispositions to such
behavior—is widespread in diverse sectors of society generally, it
is reasonable to infer that racist attitudes also exist in employment. And abundant evidence shows that overt racism is widespread today.

During the second half of the 1980s, racial violence against
blacks increased nationwide. In 1988 a white supremacist movement of violent skin-headed youths, whose weapons included
knives, baseball bats, and their own steel-toed boots, sprang up
spontaneously in cities throughout the nation. According to academic administrators, there is a "growing pattern of bigotry and
animosity towards minority students" at predominantly white
schools.[2]

Racist attitudes are also shown by the higher value juries place
on a white victim's life. One survey noted in 1986: "In the thirty-
two states where the death penalty has been imposed . . . the killer
of a white is nearly three times more likely to be sentenced to
death than the killer of a black."[3]

A landmark four-year intensive study of racism, *A Common
Destiny: Blacks and American Society* (1989), conducted by a
panel of distinguished experts, found that despite progress attitudes of racism are still widespread. There is "continuing discriminatory behavior by whites, especially in areas involving
close personal contact." Investigation of residential housing mar-
kets comparing blacks with whites of similar income shows ex-
tensive housing discrimination against blacks. Highly educated
blacks also face barriers to living in the same neighborhood with

2. *Newsweek*, January 5, 1987: 24; *Klanwatch Intelligence Report* (Mont-
gomery, Ala.: Southern Poverty Law Center, February 1989), p. 1; "Campus
Race Incidents Disquiet U. of Michigan," *New York Times*, March 9, 1987; Jon
Weiner, "Racial Hatred on Campus," *Nation*, February 27, 1989: 260–64.

3. Ronald J. Tabak, "The Death of Fairness: The Arbitrary and Capricious
Imposition of the Death Penalty in the 1980's," *Review of Law and Social
Change* 14 (1986): 826.

highly educated whites.[4] A University of Chicago investigation showed that because of persistent prejudice suburban blacks are more likely to suffer segregation than other minorities of equal income and social status. There are "strong penalties for being black."[5] The extent of housing discrimination can be gauged from a 1987 estimate by the Department of Housing and Urban Development: there are about two million instances of housing discrimination every year.[6]

According to a 1981 study black school districts in the black-belt states receive less funding and inferior education by comparison with economically similar white districts, in part as a result of local (white) decision making.[7] Black land-grant colleges and universities receive proportionately lower allotments of federal resources from the Department of Agriculture than do white institutions.[8]

Studies show that 15 to 19 percent of whites would not vote for a qualified black candidate nominated by their own party either for governor or president. According to Linda Williams, senior research associate at the Joint Center for Political Studies, their 1986 national poll showed that "the higher the office, the more whites there were who would admit that they would never vote for a black".[9]

---

4. *A Common Destiny: Blacks and American Society,* ed. Gerald David Jaynes and Robin M. Williams, Jr., for the Committee on the Status of Black Americans, Commission on Behavioral and Social Sciences and Education, National Research Council (Washington, D.C.: National Academy Press, 1989), pp. 155, 116, 140–46.

5. "Study Says Prejudice in Suburbs Is Aimed Mostly at Blacks," *New York Times,* November 23, 1988.

6. "Stepping Up the War on Discrimination," *New York Times,* November 1, 1987.

7. *A Decade of Frustrations* (Atlanta, Ga.: Southern Regional Council, 1981).

8. "Latest Charge of Racism Prompts a Debate," *New York Times,* June 30, 1986.

9. See a Joint Center for Political Studies poll reported in the *New York Times,* February 26, 1989, and Howard Schuman, Charlotte Steh, and Lawrence Bobo,

Although the percentage of whites who oppose antimiscegenation laws has risen (from 38 percent in 1963 to 66 percent in 1982), one in three whites still believes that racial intermarriage should be prohibited by law.[10]

It is implausible that racist attitudes, so widespread in contemporary society, should be significantly absent from the world of work where predominantly white employers, supervisors, and union officials decide whether blacks should be rewarded equally with whites. Although enforcement of civil rights laws in the late 1960s and 1970s deterred overt racism in the workplace, such enforcement suffered a dramatic decline after 1980, as we shall see in Chapter 2.

Institutional Racism

The neutral procedures that have had the greatest racist impact within employment are selection by (1) personal connections, (2) qualification standards, and (3) seniority status. As I shall show, although these policies may be administered by racially impartial persons, they are linked to overt racism, past, present, and future. Indeed, in some situations they serve as instruments of overt racism.

Personal Connections

Reliance by employers on friends, relatives, and neighbors— their own or their workers'—has powerful racist impact—first, because of its paramount importance in the world of work, second, because of its links to overt racism.

Racial Attitudes in America (Cambridge, Mass.: Harvard University Press, 1985), pp. 73–82.

10. Andrew Hacker, "Black Crime, White Racism," *New York Review of Books,* March 3, 1988: 38, a review of *Racial Attitudes in America.* See pp. 73–76 of that book for a report of the survey.

Numerous studies of workers—blue and white collar, professional and technical—indicate that communicating job information to family, friends, neighbors, and acquaintances by word of mouth is probably the most widely used recruitment method.[11] Vocational counselors emphasize the importance of making contacts through personal connections.[12] Academic job seekers know the value of having friends in the department of their choice. Referral unions that influence or control hiring for many well-paid jobs in such industries as construction, printing, publishing, and transportation commonly recruit through personal contacts. Kathleen Parker of the National Center for Career Strategies was reported in 1990 as stating that over 80 percent of executives find their jobs through networking and that about 86 percent of available jobs do not appear in the classified advertisements.[13] The old saying "It isn't what you know, but who you know" expresses a profound social truth.

Because, for the most part, blacks and whites live as two separate societies, it is not surprising that blacks suffer because of selection by personal contacts. Lacking ties to whites as family, friends, fellow students, neighbors, or club members, blacks tend to be isolated from the networks in which connections to desirable employment—where whites predominate—are forged.

Hence blacks have been outside the channels leading to well-paid jobs controlled by the predominantly white referral unions that recruit by word of mouth. Family or friends had virtually automatic preference for membership cards in such overwhelmingly white labor organizations as the Ironworkers' Union.[14] Such recruitment by referral unions contributed to the virtual

11. Joe R. Feagin and Clairece Booher Feagin, *Discrimination, American Style* (Englewood Cliffs, N.J.: Prentice-Hall, 1978), p. 47.

12. James M. Boros and J. Robert Parkinson, *How to Get a Fast Start in Today's Job Market* (Englewood Cliffs, N.J.: Prentice-Hall, 1980).

13. *Executive Edge* (Emmaus, Pa., August 1990).

14. Feagin, p. 50; *Affirmative Action to Open the Doors of Job Opportunity,*

exclusion of blacks from employment on public construction projects until affirmative action enforcement in the late 1960s and 1970s brought some improvement in the recruitment of minorities.

Blacks also lack personal connections to residents of all-white suburbs where many new jobs have been created. That adverse effect on blacks is exacerbated when suburban employers rely on "walk-in" applicants from these white neighborhoods.

Because whites disproportionately occupy elected government office, especially the more powerful positions, blacks suffer from the widespread use of political patronage to distribute government jobs. For example, according to the *New York Times* New York State Democratic Committee director John A. Marino said that his office funneled three thousand annual job recommendations to the state appointments office, two-thirds of which were minimum-wage seasonal positions. As the article notes, such jobs are "ideal for the children and friends of cooperative politicians."[15] And while small business has generated many of the nation's new jobs during the past decade, blacks live outside the immediate circles from which white owners tend to draw their new workers.

The handicap of exclusion from the white pipeline starts early in life. One study shows that for a young male high-school graduate, the best job route is through relatives. A 1989 comparative ethnographic study by anthropologist Mercer L. Sullivan of three neighborhood groups of young men in New York—ethnic white, hispanic, and black—showed the importance of personal connections for success in the labor market: "The labor market advantages of the . . . [white] youths over their peers in the two

Report of the Citizens' Commission on Civil Rights (Washington, D.C., 1984), p. 41; William B. Gould, *Black Workers in White Unions* (Ithaca: Cornell University Press, 1977), p. 341.

15. "Patronage Takes on Personal Touches as Parties Wane," *New York Times*, January 28, 1989.

minority neighborhoods derive not from their greater investment in human capital [e.g., education] but rather from their personal networks. These networks afford them entry into the more desirable sectors of the labor market which recruit not on the basis of education but on the basis of personal connections."[16]

Although the lack of personal connections to the job market is in most cases an institutional barrier to employment for blacks, it arises in large part from segregation created by overtly racist practices. From the period of slavery until the middle of the twentieth century, the segregation of blacks in schools, housing, accommodations, and public and private facilities was imposed by whites throughout the nation, either in ready conformity to explicitly racial laws (as in the South) or to the silent toleration of violence against blacks who dared to cross racial barriers. Today widespread segregation continues as an inherited social structure, excluding blacks from white residential areas and neighborhood schools, where they might develop white connections leading to employment. That structure of "ghettoization" is sustained by pervasive housing discrimination against blacks who wish to move into white areas.

The isolation of blacks from white society is also sustained by widespread racist attitudes that exclude blacks from white clubs and social circles where networks leading to jobs are formed. Even mild unconscious racial prejudice tends to cut blacks off from relations of friendship and intimacy with whites. A University of Chicago study of the nation's ten largest cities showed that blacks and whites rarely interact outside the workplace.[17]

Hiring by personal connections also tends to keep blacks at the

16. Juan Williams, "Racism Revisited," *Utne Reader,* May–June 1987: 56 (reprinted from the *New Republic,* November 10, 1986); Mercer L. Sullivan, "*Getting Paid*" (Ithaca: Cornell University Press, 1989), p. 226. For an analysis of the contribution made by institutions that structure the labor market to the disproportionately higher minority youth crime rate, see Sullivan, chap. 10.

17. "Study Finds Segregation in Cities Worse Than Scientists Imagined," *New York Times,* August 5, 1989.

bottom of the occupational ladder. Because individuals often hear of openings in their own kind of work, they tend to funnel such information to relatives and acquaintances. Thus both black and white workers informally recruit to *their* types of jobs. Because blacks are disproportionately represented in bottom-level positions, their personal recruitment tends to maintain occupational segregation. Continued perception of blacks in menial, undesirable jobs reinforces the racist conception that blacks belong there.

Thus, although selection by personal connections is intrinsically free of bias, its ties to overt racism—past, present, and future—justify characterization of its adverse impact on blacks as *racist impact*.

Qualification Requirements

Although black-white inequality of educational attainment has been substantially reduced in some respects, such as in the amount of schooling received and the level of reading, nevertheless requirements for a college diploma and for adequate test scores continue to exclude blacks from employment and from postgraduate schools that provide training for desirable positions.[18] Similarly, requirements for certain work experience and vague personality traits have a negative impact in employment.

Overt racism, especially in its contribution to segregating blacks from whites throughout society, makes a significant contribution to the racist impact of qualification requirements on blacks.

Millions of black persons still in the labor force today attended legally segregated public schools in seventeen southern states and

18. *A Common Destiny*, p. 332; *The Reading Report Card* (Washington, D.C.: U.S. Department of Education, Office of Educational Research and Improvement, 1990), p. 15.

the District of Columbia, where a presumption of black inferiority—destructive to their self-confidence—was pervasive, and where, because of gross discrimination in funding, black schools were invariably inferior.[19] And, as indicated earlier, a 1981 study of black-belt states shows that black school districts, by comparison with economically similar white school districts, have continued to receive less funding and inferior education, in part, as a consequence of local (white) government decisions.[20]

Many blacks are excluded by requirements for work experience because as students they had been barred from white schools where relevant training was available or had been denied work experience and training by prejudiced supervisors and employers.

In his 1979 *United Steelworkers of America v. Weber* case affidavit, Kernell Goudia, a black worker, demonstrated how past overt racism contributed to the racist impact of a "prior experience" requirement set by a Louisiana Kaiser plant for skilled jobs.

19. See Charles H. Thompson, "Problems in the Achievement of Adequate Educational Opportunity," in *Negro Education in America*, ed. Virgil A. Clift, Archibald W. Anderson and H. Gordon Hullfish (New York: Harper & Row, 1962), p. 176.

20. Underfunding of black schools is not confined to the black belt. Minority school districts in New York City have also suffered substantially from less than equal funding allocation. A 1987 study of New York City schools showed that such deprivation of educational support—repeatedly perpetrated on the poorest, overwhelmingly black and hispanic districts—extended even to resources designed to fill the urgent needs of disadvantaged students. Since there are to my knowledge no studies that compare funding to economically similar white and minority school districts (outside the black belt), conclusions as to the direct role of overt racism in such funding inequity cannot be drawn. Nevertheless, given pervasive racist attitudes, it is plausible that overt racism contributes to such inequity. But even if less than equal funding is imposed on minority school districts only because they are poor, it is undeniable that a history of overt racism has contributed substantially to the disproportionate impoverishment of blacks. Hence, as poor people, blacks suffer the racist impact of less than equal funding to poor school districts. (For information on underfunding to New York City minority school districts, see Susan Breslin with Eleanor Stier, *Promoting Poverty* [New York: Community Service Society, 1987].)

In 1968, upon discharge from the armed services, I applied to LSU trade school. I was sent an invitation to come for an interview, but when I appeared and was seen in person, I was told I would not be interviewed. Louisiana had a system of segregated trade schools, and out of the 27 schools in the state, only two accepted Blacks and their programs were limited to traditionally Black jobs. I had always been interested in getting craft training but due to discrimination was barred. I understood Kaiser had required prior experience to get into craft positions or training positions, but given the situation in Louisiana this requirement all but excluded Blacks.[21]

Overt housing discrimination affecting all economic classes of blacks works indirectly to reduce the achievement of black youngsters by contributing to the significant racial segregation of neighborhood schools.[22] The psychiatrist Stuart W. Cook informs us that studies show that desegregation in schools, "particularly when begun early and viewed cumulatively, accelerates black achievement gain."[23]

The positive effect of socialization within white families on black children's test scores is indicated in a comparative study of black children adopted by middle-class parents, white and black. The children adopted by white middle-class parents scored significantly higher on the Wechsler Intelligence Scale for Children

21. Affidavit by Kernell Goudia, sworn on May 6, 1979, and submitted to the Supreme Court for consideration in *United Steelworkers of America* v. *Weber*, 443 U.S. 193 (1979).

22. For example, in the Yonkers segregation suit the Southern District Court of New York found in 1985 that the city's housing practices, as well as city participation in school affairs, constitute "more than adequate evidence of the city's intentional perpetuation and exacerbation of racial segregation in Yonkers public schools (*United States* v. *Yonkers Board of Education,* 624 F. Supp. 1276 [S.D.N.Y. 1985])." See excerpts from the ruling by Judge Leonard B. Sand in "Judge Finds Yonkers Has Segregation Policy," *New York Times,* November 21, 1985.

23. Stuart W. Cook, "The 1954 Social Science Statement and School Desegregation: A Reply to Gerard," in *Eliminating Racism,* ed. Phyllis A. Katz and Dalmas A. Taylor (New York and London: Plenum Press, 1988), p. 248.

than did the children adopted by black middle-class parents. The scoring difference is of the magnitude "typically found between the average scores of black and white children."[24] Noting the history of segregation in the United States, John H. Fischer, past president of Columbia University's Teachers College, stated: "Every Negro child is the victim of the history of his race in this country. On the day he enters kindergarten, he carries a burden no white child can ever know."[25]

A 1989 report by the Committee on Policy for Racial Justice, chaired by the historian John Hope Franklin, points out that within the classroom teachers form "negative, inaccurate and inflexible expectations" based on the race as well as on the economic class of their students.[26] Such expectations—injurious to the motivation, self-image, and aspiration of black students— become self-fulfilling prophecies of failure in school and employment.

The racist impact of qualification requirements in employment is the terminus of a cumulative impact that begins in school. Black students are vulnerable to traditional practices such as standardized testing and tracking—that is, ability grouping in schools—which place them disproportionately at the bottom level, sometimes at a very early age, where, deprived of educational resources and instruction in higher-order skills, they have little possibility of moving up.[27]

In the job market the vulnerability of blacks to qualification requirements is exacerbated when employers insist on credentials

24. Elsie G. J. Moore, "Language Behavior in the Test Situation and the Intelligence Test Achievement of Transracially and Traditionally Adopted Black Children," in *The Language of Children Reared in Poverty*, ed. Lynne Feagans and Dale Clark Farran (New York: Academic Press, 1982), p. 152.

25. John H. Fischer, "Educational Problems of Segregation and Desegregation," in *Education in Depressed Areas*, ed. A. H. Passowe (New York: Teachers College, Columbia University, 1963), p. 291.

26. Committee on Policy for Racial Justice, *Visions of a Better Way* (Washington, D.C.: Joint Center for Political Studies Press, 1989), pp. 16–17.

27. *Visions of a Better Way*, pp. 17–18.

such as higher-education diplomas that are not related to work performance. Such requirements have had a severe effect on black employment. Irrelevant testing excluded blacks even from such dead-end work as dishwashing. In the post–Civil Rights Act period, the U.S. Equal Employment Opportunity Commission discovered that employers almost uniformly failed to establish that employment requirements reliably measured ability to do the job. The Wonderlic Test, probably the most widely used general intelligence test in industry, had practically no significant value in predicting industrial job performance.[28]

The adverse effect of irrelevant higher education requirements increases when, as in the recessions of the 1970s, college graduates were willing to take traditionally black jobs or, as in 1990, when college graduates—in oversupply—were being hired as clerks, bookeepers, and so forth.[29]

An important race-neutral qualification standard in the academic marketplace is published research. Taking Harvard University as an example, sociologist Thomas Pettigrew shows how this requirement adversely affects black candidates. In the 1930s, Harvard developed criteria for tenured faculty appointment, which included scholarly publication. The purpose was to ensure a faculty of high quality. Publication requirements, however, worked against the recruitment of black professors because the majority taught heavy course loads in predominantly black colleges, which limited their time for research and writing.[30] This concentration of blacks in predominantly black colleges has links

28. Sources on invalid qualification requirements: "Legal Implications of the Use of Standardized Ability Tests in Employment and Education," *Columbia Law Review* 68 (1968): 691, 701; George Cooper and Richard B. Sobol, "Seniority and Testing under Fair Employment Laws: A General Approach to Objective Criteria of Hiring and Promotion," *Harvard Law Review* 82 (June 1969): 1644.

29. See Louis Uchitelle, "Surplus of College Graduates Dims Job Outlook for Others," *New York Times,* June 18, 1990.

30. Thomas F. Pettigrew, "Racism and the Mental Health of White Ameri-

to a racist past, because black academics were initially excluded by racist attitudes from many white departments. Hence in the 1970s, when some predominantly white universities following affirmative action requirements sought black professors, black college faculty were less able to fill their race-neutral publication requirements.

Although qualification requirements are intrinsically bias-free, they can be manipulated by racist employers and union officials to exclude blacks. Thus while some employers who set irrelevant higher education requirements may simply have undue reverence for diplomas, many are not unhappy that their requirements tend to keep blacks out. According to one legal scholar, raising qualification criteria has been a "common device of employers and construction unions" when, because of civil rights law, hiring and promotion of blacks appeared likely.[31]

Tests plainly not germane to job performance have served the same racist purpose. A classic instance was the attempt by an Ironworkers' local to bar Howard Lewis, a black welder with thirty years' experience, by insisting that he pass a newly introduced and irrelevant knot-tying test.[32]

Vague subjective standards, such as "fitting in," "personality," "vigor," and "self-confidence"—widely used for promotion—easily serve racial prejudice. In *Rowe* v. *General Motors Co.*, the court stated that promotion procedures that depend on "subjective evaluation" by immediate supervisors are a "ready mechanism" for covert race discrimination. The court expressed skepticism that blacks, dependent on whites for decisive recommendation, can expect impartiality.[33]

cans: A Social Psychological View," in *Racism in Mental Health*, ed. Charles V. Willie, Bernard M. Kramer, and Bertram S. Brown (Pittsburgh, Pa.: University of Pittsburgh Press, 1973), p. 275.

31. Albert W. Blumrosen, *Black Employment and the Law* (New Brunswick, N.J.: Rutgers University Press, 1971), p. 32.

32. Gould, pp. 479–80.

33. 457 F.2d 348 (5th Cir. 1972); reported by Gould, p. 291.

Seniority Systems

Seniority status determines promotion, layoff, and job termination for vast numbers of employees: professionals, managers, clericals, skilled, and unskilled workers. A *Harvard Law Review* report states that seniority is one of "the most important bastions of status in our economy": "Enshrined in countless collective bargaining agreements, seniority occupies a unique position in American labor relations."[34]

Seniority systems have brought significant benefits to American workers. Promotion based on seniority enables harmony, cooperation, and solidarity to replace an ugly scramble for advancement over one's co-workers. Seniority-determined layoff protects workers against arbitrary dismissal due to an employer's whim, malice, or prejudice. Strengthened by such security, many workers have gained in dignity and self-esteem and are less tempted to pander to supervisors or accept humiliating conditions. An older auto worker told me that before the union had negotiated a seniority system his supervisor would invite subordinates over on Sunday to mow his lawn. With the protection of a seniority system, workers can demand to be treated with a measure of respect. Egalitarian philosophers, that is, those committed to equal economic reward, may note that seniority-based benefit systems constitute a significant egalitarian substructure in the hierarchy of employment. Insofar as seniority determines promotion, pay, and job security, protected employees tend to gain equally throughout their working lives.

But seniority, in itself race-neutral, has disproportionately benefited white workers. Hired in most cases ahead of blacks, whites have enjoyed higher seniority status.[35] Blacks felt the racist impact of such past hiring discrimination when, as less senior, they

34. "Employment Discrimination and the Title VII of the Civil Rights Act of 1964," *Harvard Law Review* 84 (1971): 1156.
35. Philip S. Foner, *Organized Labor and the Black Worker, 1619–1973* (New York: Praeger, 1974), p. 427.

were less likely to gain promotion and more likely to lose their jobs in economic recessions. As we shall see, even in industries where blacks entered early, those who achieved high seniority status often suffered the racist impact of departmental seniority arrangements, which locked them into the most miserable jobs.

In the 1970s blacks, hired under affirmative action programs in private and public employment (e.g., as teachers, police, and firefighters), were devastated by seniority-based layoffs—a consequence of three recessions and severe government budget cutbacks.[36] Such layoffs threaten minorities again in the 1990s.

As job losers, blacks tend to move down to unskilled temporary work, or to no work at all. This downward move is facilitated by their lack of significant financial assets, which often makes job retraining unfeasible.[37] Whites have eleven times the wealth of blacks; one-third of all blacks have no major assets whatsoever except for cash on hand.[38] Thus seniority-based layoffs of blacks, including those hired because of affirmative action programs, increases the concentration of blacks at the bottom of the occupational ladder or among the unemployed, thereby reinforcing the racist stereotype of blacks as inferior.

Although long-term black employees have the benefit of high seniority ranking, after the 1964 Civil Rights Act many continued to suffer the racist impact of departmental seniority arrangements. Under such arrangements, a worker who transfers from one department to another loses all seniority credit. Although departmental seniority is a race-neutral practice, it per-

36. *Last Hired, First Fired: Layoffs and Civil Rights* (Washington, D.C.: U.S. Commission on Civil Rights, 1977), pp. 10–25. The disproportionately high rate of minority job loss due to seniority-based layoff during the 1970s, in both the private and public sector, is documented in this 1977 report: "In some areas where minorities represented only 10–12% of the work force they accounted for 60–70% of those being laid off in 1974" (pp. 24–25). The commission concluded that the "continuing implementation of layoffs by seniority inevitably means the gutting of affirmative action efforts in employment" (p. 61).

37. *Last Hired, First Fired*, p. 14.

38. "Whites Own 11 Times the Assets Blacks Have, Census Study Finds," *New York Times*, July 19, 1986.

petuates the victimizing effect of past overtly racist job assignment. Newly hired blacks in northern and southern plants had traditionally been assigned to segregated departments where they labored in the most undesirable, low-paying jobs, for example, at garbage disposal, the blast furnaces and the coke ovens, and in the foundries. After the 1964 Civil Rights Act, black workers could no longer be legally prevented from transfer to the better, white departments. But under departmental seniority arrangements, transfers were stripped of all seniority, and so they descended to the bottom rung for promotion and layoff. Thus blacks naturally tended to remain in the racially segregated departments, where they had originally been assigned by biased company supervisors.

Summary: The Ties of Race-Neutral Procedures to Overt Racism

Overt racism, past and present, contributes to social and residential segregation, thereby isolating blacks at every income level from white society. Because of such isolation, blacks are vulnerable, by exclusion, to selection by personal connections. The negative impact of qualification standards in employment is sustained by racially biased funding of education and training resources and by the cumulative racist impact of such practices as tracking in schools. Blacks suffer the adverse effects of seniority-based promotion and layoff because of past racist hiring of whites ahead of blacks.

Institutional racism also reinforces future racism by contributing to the disproportionate presence of blacks at the bottom of employment—a presence that helps perpetuate the racist attitude that blacks are inherently inferior. White notions of black people have been formed in a social world where blacks visibly predominate at these bottom levels. Thus they have labored—and continue to labor—as maids and porters, at "hot, heavy, and dirty" jobs in the foundries and paint pits of the auto plants, the boiler rooms of utilities, the dusty basements of tobacco factories, and in the murderous heat of the steel mills' coke ovens. Today, while some blacks have moved on up, it is still true that the more disagreeable the job, the greater the chance of finding a high proportion of blacks doing it. In 1984, Herman Schwartz, a legal scholar, noted that blacks constitute over 50 percent of the nation's maids and garbage collectors, but only 4 percent of its managers and 3 percent of its physicians and lawyers.[39] The racially exclusionary impact of race-neutral policies on employment also contributes to the official black unemployment rate as perpetually double that of whites, thereby reenforcing the racist view of blacks as unwilling to work. Thus these race-neutral policies function as social mechanisms through which the victimizing effects of overt racism, past and present, continue to keep blacks at the bottom levels of employment.

Postscript: In 1991, when this book was in proof, the Urban Institute published the results of an investigation of overt race discrimination in employment. Testers—equally qualified young black and white men, articulate and conventionally dressed—applied through newspaper advertisements for entry-level jobs in Chicago and Washington, D.C. The results showed "widespread and pervasive" race discrimination against young black males. Such discrimination appeared greatest in jobs offering the best wages and future income potential. The investigators concluded that race discrimination contributes to black male unemployment and nonparticipation in the labor force. See Margery Austin Turner, Michael Fix, and Raymond J. Struyk, *Opportunities Denied, Opportunities Diminished: Discrimination in Hiring* (Washington, D.C.: The Urban Institute, 1991) pp. 32–33.

39. Herman Schwartz, "Affirmative Action," in *Minority Report,* ed. Leslie W. Dunbar (New York: Pantheon Books, 1984), p. 61.

2

Remedies for Racism

In assessing the remedies for racism, I will be concerned not with legal issues (e.g., whether these remedies are compatible with the Constitution) but rather with their practical effectiveness and moral acceptability. The development of legal remedies in the 1960s and 1970s, in conformity with the 1964 Civil Rights Act and a federal executive order, provides an instructive context for such assessment.

The Complaint Remedy for Overt Discrimination

Actions taken to remedy overt discrimination against identifiable individuals may be referred to, broadly speaking, as complaints. These complaints can be lodged in a court or administrative agency under Title 7 of the 1964 Civil Rights Act, which prohibits such discrimination, and may be pursued against a firm or a union on behalf of an identifiable individual or group. A class-action suit claiming salary or promotion discrimination against all class members, such as all minority workers in a firm, exemplifies a group complaint. If overt hiring or promotion discrimination is proved, the employer is required to remedy the violation, usually by hiring or promoting the complainant or, in the case of salary discrimination, by awarding back pay.

While complaint remedies satisfy a reasonable claim for restitution, they are deficient in a number of ways. First, they are often not practical even in obvious cases of racial bias. Victims are frequently reluctant to complain because workers who assert their rights are labeled troublemakers. (Many of the rights we now take for granted were won by troublemakers.) That label can damage a person—especially a black person—for her entire working life. A realistic assessment of such damage to themselves and the families they support often stops black people from initiating justified complaints.

Second, the blacks who do file complaints must prove that their employer acted out of racial bias. Such bias appears evident when no alternative explanation for racially unequal pay is plausible, but in other situations management frequently has effective strategies for covering up racial bias.

How does a black applicant know whether the job has really "just been filled"? How can an experienced black worker demonstrate that the announcement of a managerial opening was canceled because the employer learned that she—a *black* employee—was clearly the best-qualified candidate? Also, firms can enlist the cooperation of employment agencies in concealing behind-the-scenes discrimination. The difficulty of proving bias, when employers often have the power to conceal such prejudice, reduces the effectiveness of the complaint remedy.

A similar problem confronts a black person who seeks housing in white areas where jobs are available. Landlords and realtors, like employers, have effective strategies for defeating complaints of racial prejudice. Does a black apartment-seeker have proof—

or the time to assemble proof—that a landlord's excuses ("The apartment isn't available because it needs repair") are conjured up to exclude blacks, or that a real estate agent is steering black clients away from white neighborhoods?

Since the complaint remedy requires proof of bias, it does not apply to institutional race-neutral policies. Yet qualification standards can be manipulated by prejudiced employers to exclude blacks, especially, as we have seen, vague personality standards. Decisive proof of bias is frequently not obtainable in such cases.

Where employers hire by personal connections, blacks isolated by segregation from white society are unaware of job openings. Having never applied, these segregated blacks have no grounds for filing a discrimination complaint. Hence segregation contributes to the inadequacy of the complaint remedy.

The complaint remedy is also irrelevant to the racist impact of impartially applied qualification standards that sustain the victimizing effects of past racism, such as the underfunding of segregated black schools and the refusal of employers and unions to hire and train black workers. Absent racism, there would have been, statistically speaking, a racial redistribution of workers; *some* blacks moving up, *some* whites moving down. But those blacks and those whites cannot be identified as individuals. Yet the blacks, so victimized, are out there in the world of work, real persons still suffering the effects of racist injury.

While complaints are an inadequate tool for overcoming racism, especially institutional racism, they nevertheless can be financially burdensome to employers because they require payment of legal fees and, in some cases, back-pay settlements. These costs increase when back pay is awarded to a group of employees who have brought a class-action suit. As we shall see in the next section, an employer strategy for preventing such suits turned out to be the remedy for institutional discrimination—affirmative action.

Affirmative Action—The Background

My analysis of affirmative action focuses primarily on its practice before 1980; after this time, as we shall see, the federal government's impetus to enforce and sustain affirmative action declined substantially.

Broadly speaking, affirmative action (hereafter AA) consists not merely of passive nondiscrimination but of active measures to increase significantly the recruitment and upgrading of minorities. Blacks are not required, as in the complaint remedy, to prove an employer's overt discrimination against them; hence a crucial weakness of the complaint remedy is eliminated.

Both before and after the federal government initiated AA requirements, civil rights organizations pursued boycotts, picketing, wild cat strikes, and demonstrations that brought direct pressure on employers and unions for recruiting, training, and upgrading more blacks. Among these groups were People United to Serve Humanity (OPERATION PUSH), the Committee on Racial Equality (CORE), the Dodge Revolutionary Union Movement (DRUM), a Detroit-based, militant, and sometimes violence-prone black auto-worker group, and the United Construction Workers' Association (UCWA), a Seattle-based black-worker organization.

In 1964 the A&P made an agreement with CORE, stating that 90 percent of its new employees for the following year would be nonwhite.[1] In 1968, DRUM called for the hiring of additional black foremen in auto plants. In 1972, after a court ordered Seattle craft unions to increase their black apprentices, UCWA closed down construction projects to speed up compliance with the court order.[2] No doubt such activity by the civil rights move-

1. Augie Meier, "Civil Rights Strategies for Employment," in *Employment, Race and Poverty,* ed. Arthur M. Ross and Herbert Hill (New York: Harcourt Brace and World, 1967), p. 198.
2. William B. Gould, *Black Workers in White Unions* (Ithaca: Cornell University Press, 1977), pp. 345–51.

ment contributed to the development of government-sanctioned AA in the 1960s and early 1970s.[3]

AA was targeted to reduce the adverse effects in employment of past and present racist practices. As we have seen, such practices include segregated education, housing discrimination in areas of available employment, the last-hired, first-fired policies of employers which deprived blacks of seniority and work experience, the exclusion of blacks from white society where personal connections to jobs are made, and the refusal of unions and firms to train black youths. The effects of such racist practices show up in the statistical overrepresentation of blacks at the bottom of the occupational ladder and among the unemployed. AA aimed to diminish these effects by moving the black work force toward approximate statistical parity—that is, to achieve occupational integration throughout the hierarchy of employment. It is true that, absent a racist past, such statistical parity might not now exist everywhere in employment. But although a past without racism cannot be reconstructed, we do know that when occupational integration is finally achieved, the significant effects in employment of that invidious history will in large part be gone. Moreover, persons who mature in a society where the upper employment levels are racially integrated will be less likely to assume that blacks belong at the bottom.

Some courts and government civil rights agencies, construing statistical underrepresentation of blacks in sectors of employment as the continuing effect of a racist past, have perceived AA recruitment as a means of eradicating such underrepresentation. They also became aware, however, that such efforts to hire and

3. Herbert Hammerman writes: "By 1968 . . . voluntary programs had made no significant change in employment practices [for blacks]. . . . There were strong pressures on the government to produce results. Urban riots, increasing civil rights militance, the promise of the 'Great Society' programs, all contributed to a sense of urgency to show immediate results" (*A Decade of New Opportunity: Affirmative Action in the 1970's* [Washington D.C.: Potomac Institute, 1984], p. 14).

upgrade minorities were consistently blocked by the adverse racial impact of neutral selection practices which continued to preserve white predominance, especially in desirable positions. Hence, as a number of government agencies and courts have recognized, increased recruitment of blacks requires that reasonable strategies be devised to reduce institutional discrimination, that is, to lessen the racist impact of employment neutrals: selection by personal connections, qualification requirements, and seniority status. A 1984 report by the Citizens' Commission on Civil Rights sums up that story: "[These AA remedies] grew out of the persistent use of practices such as word-of-mouth recruiting, 'old boy' networks, aptitude and other tests not related to job performance which continued to prevent the employment of minorities and women even after overt practices of discrimination had ended."[4]

Thus, while employment neutrals have functioned as social mechanisms that perpetuate the victimizing effects of past and present racist injury, AA in employment has become the social remedy that is designed to reduce that racist impact in the workplace. Let us examine AA from that perspective.

Unspecific vs. Specific AA:
Good Faith vs. Numerical Goals

As we have seen, selection by personal connections tends to favor whites at the expense of blacks. Outreach to minority candidates seemed an obvious way to remedy the racist impact of such selection. It is important to distinguish two ways in which such outreach can be conducted: First, there are "good faith" efforts to recruit blacks, made without numerical goals or time-

---

4. *Affirmative Action to Open the Doors of Job Opportunity,* Report of the Citizens' Commission on Civil Rights (Washington, D.C., 1984), p. 10.

tables for hiring them. This method exemplifies *unspecific* AA. Second, there are good faith efforts capped by definite, dated numerical targets. The second illustrates *specific* AA.

Unspecific outreach efforts include advertising positions and recruitment visits to black schools.[5] Such visits to minorities exemplify a *purely racial* remedy since they benefit only minorities. Advertising positions, however, is a *quasi-racial* remedy since it also benefits those whites who, excluded from behind-the-scenes hiring networks, learn about job openings through such advertising.

The seriousness of unspecific outreach, uncapped by dated numerical targets, depends on the determination of the employer or surrogate—such as a referral union—to direct jobs toward blacks, hence away from whites. Without pressure for recruiting a definite number of blacks, however, the employer can go through the motions of AA and hire only a token number or none at all. The fact is that unspecific outreach is simply insufficient. Resistance to breaking comfortable recruitment habits that substantially benefit one's friends, family, and so forth is predictable.

The need for specific AA in academia—where the traditional "old boy" system draws graduate-school friends into one's department family—was noted in 1975 by Harold C. Fleming, president of the Potomac Institute: "A high degree of specificity . . . is the only way affirmative action can . . . be meaningfully monitored. . . . It is no indictment of the morality of professors to suggest that they share our common human frailty in finding it difficult to change old habits and ingrained practices without pressure from, and accountability to, authority outside our own comfortable peer group."[6]

5. Taking race as a factor for professional-school admission also exemplifies unspecific AA. See *Regents of University of California* v. *Bakke,* 438 U.S. 267 (1978).

6. Statement by Harold G. Fleming at a consultation sponsored by the U.S. Commission on Civil Rights in 1975 (*Affirmative Action in Employment in Higher Education,* [Washington, D.C.: United States Commission on Civil Rights, 1975], p. 23).

Generally speaking, where resistance is expected or extra effort required—as when a person plans to save money or a firm decides to increase production—the effectiveness of definite, dated goals is recognized. In collective bargaining, unions demand not vague employer promises to try to raise wages but definite, contractually binding pay increases.

In firms where desirable positions have formerly been filled by personal connections, effective AA can divert good jobs from one's white contacts and give them to blacks. In such situations, vague outreach efforts without definite numerical goals are bound to be inadequate. Such efforts will also be insufficient in situations where hiring procedures—whatever they are—can be manipulated by prejudiced personnel officers. Lack of specificity invites evasion. Moreover, even impartial employers find unspecific outreach requirements difficult to administer. Without definite numerical targets, they have no standard of reasonable progress in the recruitment of minorities.

The practical necessity for dated numerical targets became obvious to federal investigators monitoring the AA efforts of government contractors in the 1960s and 1970s. They found that entrenched habits of dispensing positions, especially desirable ones, to personal connections often paralyzed minority outreach.

For example, the Kaiser Aluminum and Chemical Company, located in a 39-percent black Louisiana area, had an only 9-percent-black work force. A "white pipeline" had worked to exclude blacks from the relatively well-paid positions in this United Steelworkers–organized plant. A significant breakthrough for blacks was made, however, in the early 1970s by the implementation of a 50-percent-minority hiring goal for production workers and in 1974 by the establishment of a 50-percent-minority craft training program.[7]

In the building trades, craft-union members' preference for

---

7. Gertrude Ezorsky, "The Case of the Missing Evidence," *Washington Post Outlook*, May 27, 1979.

their white personal contacts for top-paying apprenticeships was virtually automatic until AA was introduced in the late 1960s and 1970s. A case indicating the need for numerical goals involved the Los Angeles Steam Fitters Local #250. Not a single nonwhite held a card in this union of three thousand members. The local made no serious move to bring in black apprentices until 1972, when the Justice Department insisted on dated numerical goals. The three previous years of "good faith" efforts had accomplished nothing."[8]

In the Philadelphia area in 1969, after eight years of supposed commitment during the 1960s to equal opportunity with little result, government construction contractors were ordered by the U.S. Department of Labor to set minority numerical goals.[9] The Philadelphia Plan, which incorporated these goals, had national repercussions for the construction industry, as legal scholar William B. Gould describes: "The winds of Philadelphia were being felt throughout the land. The belief that the unions and contractors had obligations to recruit minorities, obligations which could be effected only if 'goals' and 'timetables' for minority hiring were established, was reflected both in the acceleration of black demands and in a new-found inclination by the white building trades and contractors to negotiate plans. For the first time, a climate which favored meaningful efforts to alleviate employment discrimination was beginning to develop."[10]

These cases illustrate the need for numerical remedies in firms and industries where recruitment by personal connections had been practiced. Numerical targets also act as a powerful deterrent against overt racism. A racist employer under pressure to hire a definite number of blacks will hesitate before victimizing a black applicant. When we appraise AA remedies for neutral selection practices, the importance of goals and timetables will again be evident.

8. Gould, p. 322.
9. *Affirmative Action to Open the Doors*, pp. 45–48.
10. Gould, pp. 339–40.

Government civil rights agencies and the courts have played a major role in developing numerical remedies. Their authority for establishing such remedies derives mainly from two sources: First, Executive Order 11246 guidelines (1971) require that dated numerical targets for hiring, training, and promoting minorities be set by firms that hold government contracts but have underutilized minorities, that is, have employed fewer than "would reasonably be expected by their availability."[11] Employers who fail to meet their numerical goals but can demonstrate "good faith" efforts are not subject to loss of government contracts. Second, Title 7 of the 1964 Civil Rights Act empowers the courts to order such "affirmative action as may be appropriate" for relief of past discrimination.[12] Consequently, courts have issued powerful judicial decrees, such as the AT&T consent decree and the Steel Industry Settlement, mandating numerical targets for reducing minority underutilization.[13] Because courts have construed such reduction by employers as evidence that past discrimination is being remedied, firms seeking to prevent costly Title 7 suits have, as voluntary affirmative action, established numerical goals.

In some situations where blacks are notoriously scarce, the courts have approved "set-asides," which unlike goals, reserve a specific number of positions for minorities only. Whites are excluded from competing for such positions. A 10-percent government contract set-aside for minority-owned firms was upheld by the Supreme Court in *Fullilove* v. *Klutznick* (1980).[14] In black-owned firms hiring by personal connections tends to benefit blacks. Hence government contract set-asides for minority firms are bound to increase black employment.

While the moral problems raised by AA will be discussed in

11. U.S. Department of Labor, Office of Federal Contract Compliance, 60-2-11(a), *Federal Register* 36 (December 4, 1971).

12. 42 U.S.C. #2000e *et seq.*

13. *Affirmative Action to Open the Doors*, pp. 59–61.

14. *Fullilove v. Klutznick* 448 U.S. 448 (1980).

Part II, it will be useful at this point to clarify one issue concerning numerical remedies which has moral import. Some analysts refer to numerical remedies as "quotas"; however, that label should be avoided. It is true that a numerical goal (or set-aside) does not differ, semantically speaking, from a numerical quota. Nevertheless, tagging AA numerical remedies as "quotas" is misleading, for that label suggests that such AA measures are relevantly similar to the old quotas that decades ago excluded many Jews from professional schools. But the old exclusionary quotas against Jews were motivated by a false, derogatory notion of their social inferiority, a notion that defined Jews as pushy, vulgar, and mercenary. Those quotas aimed to maintain a professional society restricted by such immoral bias—a society dominated by Christian gentlemen. In contrast, an important purpose of AA numerical remedies is occupational integration, a workplace society where biased stereotypes of blacks as inferior have largely been dissipated. To tag such AA measures as quotas falsely suggests that they, like yesterday's quotas, serve an immoral end.

Presumably, AA critics who use the quota label pejoratively believe that numerical remedies serve an immoral purpose. That conclusion requires demonstration by argument, and the quota label is not a substitute for such argument.

AA and Qualification Requirements

How does AA reduce the racist impact of qualification criteria?

As we have seen, competence requirements that are not related to performance on the job have severely handicapped blacks in employment. A specific remedy—*validation of qualification requirements*—was developed by the Equal Employment Opportunity Commission (EEOC), which is the executive agency that administers Title 7, and it was upheld by the Supreme Court in

Griggs v. *Duke Power Co.* (1971): When a qualification standard excludes blacks disproportionately, the employer is required to validate the standard, to demonstrate that it fairly measures ability to perform the job.

In 1966 the EEOC first issued guidelines stating that employers whose qualification criteria disproportionately exclude minorities violate the Civil Rights Act unless they can demonstrate that the requirement does in fact fairly determine job-related skills. Detailed testing guidelines were then published by the EEOC in 1970. For evaluation of job-ability testing, the EEOC relied on standards established by such professional organizations as the American Psychological Association.[15]

In *Griggs,* the Supreme Court unanimously endorsed the EEOC's testing guidelines:

> *The Civil Rights Act proscribes not only overt discrimination, but practices that are fair in form, but discriminatory in operation. The touchstone is business necessity.* If an employment practice which operates to exclude Negroes cannot be shown to be related to job performance, the practice is prohibited. On the record before us neither the high school completion requirement nor the general intelligence test is shown to bear a demonstrable relation to successful performance on the jobs for which it is used. Both were adopted, as the Court of Appeals noted, without meaningful study of their relationship to job-performance ability. . . . The evidence, however, shows that employees who have not completed high school or taken the tests have continued to perform satisfactorily and make progress in departments for which the high school and test criteria are now used. . . . *Because they are Negroes, petitioners have long received inferior education in seg-*

15. *Oversight Hearing on EEOC's Proposed Modification of Enforcement Regulations, Including Uniform Guidelines on Employee Selection Procedures,* Hearings before the Subcommittee on Employment Opportunities of the Committee on Education and Labor, House of Representatives (Washington, D.C.: U.S. Government Printing Office, 1986), pp. 98–100.

regated schools . . . good intent or absence of discriminatory intent does not redeem employment procedures or testing mechanisms that operate as "built-in headwinds" for minority groups and are unrelated to measuring job capability. (emphases added)[16]

Note that according to *Griggs* the Civil Rights Act ban on discrimination applies not only to overt discrimination, which requires biased intent, but also to neutral practices, such as tests, which are "fair in form, but discriminatory in operation." As the court suggests, the "built-in headwinds" for blacks, exemplified by neutral testing mechanisms, emanate from past racist practices, such as inferior segregated education, which have racist impact in employment. Thus in this historic decision the Supreme Court extended the concept of discrimination to include institutional as well as overt discrimination.

As a consequence of *Griggs,* a number of employers whose qualification criteria tended to exclude minorities either validated their requirements or developed alternative standards that reduced disparate minority impact. Some employers have relied on relevant demonstrated ability to learn complex tasks. Some large national companies have substituted work-related requirements in lieu of paper-and-pencil tests for blue-collar positions.[17]

The use of job-related criteria can also identify minority persons with borderline qualifications but who, with relevant skill training, can become competent workers. Training such "qualifiable" black workers is an important part of AA.

Reasonable alternatives to college-diploma requirements (which adversely affect blacks) are available in many situations.

---

16. *Griggs* v. *Duke Power Co.,* 401 U.S. 424 (1971).

17. Richard T. Seymour, "Challenging a Test: What Plaintiffs' Counsel Look for in Deciding Whether to Prosecute a Case" (draft copyright, 1987); and information based on telephone interview with Richard T. Seymour, January 1988.

Recent studies show that less-educated workers can be trained by employers for skilled positions that are frequently reserved for college graduates.[18]

Employers who perceive a higher-education degree as an indicator of good work habits frequently use it as a sorting mechanism for low-skilled jobs because college graduates—now in oversupply—are often available for such positions. Some employers, however, have effectively used alternatives to the college diploma, such as probationary periods for permanent jobs and sophisticated applicant-screening techniques, for determining work habits. Such procedures together with training for "qualifiable" blacks can be incorporated into AA programs.

Where measures to increase minority employment are too costly for employers, I suggest in Part II that federal subsidies be made available to them.

The "Basically Qualified" Strategy

In some situations in which blacks are severely underrepresented, meeting a numerical goal may require selecting a specific number of blacks who are "basically qualified" to do the job, rather than choosing the best-qualified candidates who are white. Such preference was explicitly permitted by the landmark court-ordered agreement between AT&T, the EEOC, and the departments of Labor and Justice in 1973.[19] Also the EEOC's 1979

18. See Louis Uchitelle, "Surplus of College Graduates Dims Job Outlook for Others," *New York Times*, June 18, 1990. In transferring employees from older factories to new high-tech plants, Motorola, Inc., found that many workers who failed a basic-skills test that required an eighth-grade reading level and knowledge of fractions could master these skills after six months in company-sponsored remedial classes. These workers were then ready for on-the-job training.

19. *Equal Employment Opportunity Commission v. American Telephone & Telegraph et al.*, No. 73–149 (E.D. Pa. Jan. 18, 1973). A similar type of prefer-

guidelines for voluntary affirmative action recommend that, in devising numerical goals, employers take into account the availability of "basically qualified" minority persons.[20]

A comprehensive appraisal of the moral criticisms of preferential treatment is undertaken in Part II. At this point, however, a relevant semantic issue with moral import should be clarified. Some analysts characterize whites who are excluded by AA racial preference as objects of reverse discrimination. But such characterization suggests—incorrectly—that the overt racism blacks have suffered is now being inflicted on these white candidates. A candidate rejected because of race, however, is not necessarily an object of overt racism. Suppose an actor is denied the part of Othello because he is white. Although he is deliberately rejected because of his race, such treatment does not exemplify racial bias. Hence he is not a victim of overt racism. Similarly, a white candidate excluded by a racially preferential program is not subjected to racially prejudiced treatment. His rejection is not based on a derogatory false notion of racial inferiority; thus he is not a victim of overt racism, even in reverse. It is still possible that the exclusion of this white candidate exemplifies some *other* kind of unfairness. I assess that claim in Part II.

Basically Qualified Academic Candidates

Should academic institutions extend hiring preference to basically qualified black candidates? The sad fact is that black students in most colleges rarely see a black instructor. Such occupational segregation reinforces a black youth's perception of

---

ence was endorsed in *Johnson v. Santa Clara Transportation Agency* 107 S.Ct. 1442 (1987). The court upheld promotion of a woman over a "marginally better qualified" male, pursuant to an AA plan providing that race or sex could be considered when there was a need to "remedy underrepresentation" (*Academe*, September–October 1987).

20. *Affirmative Action to Open the Doors*, p. 64.

academic society as a white preserve. A college with a preferential hiring policy would hire black instructors who, although in some situations less qualified than white candidates, are nevertheless competent to teach and carry on research in their field. Such preference for blacks in recruiting college teachers can contribute to racial integration of faculties, but given the scarcity of blacks as Ph.D.'s—only 2.6 percent of 1986 Ph.D.'s were awarded to blacks—reliance on that strategy alone would not achieve sufficient progress.[21] Howard Glickstein, former counsel to the U.S. Civil Rights Commission, offers a relevant observation:

> You have to consider people that are trainable [even without Ph.D.'s], people that are in the graduate schools, people that are available. . . . I find it somewhat peculiar to hear universities complain about lack of qualified people. It's one thing for General Electric to say there is a lack of qualified engineers, but it is the universities themselves that provide the credentials for university employment, and they can certainly be expected to do better.[22]

As Glickstein suggests, universities through their graduate programs are strategically situated to train blacks as college teachers. A specific number of places could be set aside for black applicants who are basically qualified for graduate study. These students could serve as teaching assistants or part-time instructors, college teachers in training. Employment of graduate students as apprentice teachers is, in fact, now widely practiced in universities and colleges.

By significantly expanding the pool of black candidates quali-

21. S. L. Coyle and Y. Bae, *Summary Report, 1986: Doctoral Recipients from United States Universities* (Washington, D.C.: National Research Council, 1987); cited in Dionne J. Jones, Eva W. Chunn, and Stephanie G. Robinson, "Education: In Search of Equity and Excellence," in *Black Americans and Public Policy* (New York: National Urban League, 1988), p. 46.

22. Quoted in *Affirmative Action in Employment in Higher Education*, p. 46.

43

fied for employment as college teachers, AA preferential programs for both training and hiring black teachers would constitute an important step toward racial integration of academic faculty.

Remedies for Racial Impact of Seniority-Based Layoff: Work-Sharing and Preferential Treatment

As noted earlier, blacks recently hired by government and private industry under AA plans suffered the impact of seniority-based layoffs in the 1970s—a consequence of three recessions and government budget cutbacks. Such layoffs are expected again in the 1990s.

One significant remedy for reducing that impact—work-sharing—was advocated by both the U.S. Commission on Civil Rights (1977) and the Equal Employment Opportunity Commission (1980).[23] The following hypothetical case illustrates the practice: Suppose that for decades Smith and Co. had been a virtually all-white plant, but because of AA requirements it hired a number of black workers. Now a business recession mandates a one-fifth layoff. Because seniority determines layoff, blacks, as most recently hired, would be the first to go, and the work force would once again become almost all white. A work-sharing remedy would avoid that consequence. All employees would be placed on a four day-week. As a California law has allowed, they could collect unemployment compensation for the fifth day. This remedy has the virtue of fairness since it distributes the layoff burden over the entire work force. In Chapter 4, I suggest other measures that, like work-sharing, distribute the layoff burden more equitably over employees.

A different kind of AA remedy, which focuses not on spreading

23. *Last Hired, First Fired: Layoffs and Civil Rights* (Washington, D.C.: U.S. Commission on Civil Rights, 1977), pp. 49–54; Eleanor Holmes Norton, "Layoffs and Equal Employment Opportunity," *Federal Register* 45 (September 12, 1980).

the impact of layoff but only on keeping minority employees, is racial preference in retention. If Smith & Co. gave such preferential treatment to their black workers in implementing the one-fifth layoff, one-fifth of the whites and (only) one-fifth of the blacks would be laid off by seniority within their racial group. As a consequence, some more senior whites would be laid off while some less senior blacks would retain their jobs. The plant would remain—as immediately before the layoff—one-fifth black.

In *Vulcan Pioneers* v. *New Jersey Department of Civil Service* (1984), Federal District Court Judge H. Lee Sarokin devised such a preferential seniority remedy for municipal budgetary layoff of minority firefighters, who like their counterparts in cities throughout the land had been recruited under AA plans to a predominantly white force. He stated, however, that because the more senior white firefighters would be giving up their jobs "in the name of the public good" the public should assume financial responsibility, and he ordered that these white firefighters be compensated. Since the layoff was instituted because of a municipal budgetary crisis, he ruled that the compensation be paid by the federal government.[24] However, as we shall see, because of a Supreme Court ruling in another seniority-based layoff case, *(Firefighters* v. *Stotts)* Judge Sarokin was required to withdraw his federal district court order in June 1984.[25]

Glickstein cites a historical precedent indicating that compen-

24. *Vulcan Pioneers* v. *New Jersey Department of Civil Service*, 34 Fair Empl. Prac. Cas. (BNA) 1239 (D.N.J. 1984). Ira Glasser suggests that whites who are adversely affected by racial preference in layoff might be compensated by their *employers*, who are responsible for the past hiring discrimination that resulted in higher seniority for whites ("Affirmative Action and Racial Injustice," *Eliminating Racism*, p. 352).

Although this proposal is not implausible, in practice it would have an undesirable consequence. Recently hired blacks would become a monetary liability for firms in layoff situations. Employers would be required to retain them and pay compensation to the more senior whites who would be laid off instead. Since hiring blacks now might prove financially burdensome later, employers would be reluctant to recruit them. This consequence should be avoided.

25. *Firefighters Local Union No. 1784* v. *Stotts* 467 U.S. 561 (1984).

sating affected white workers may reduce their opposition to preferential treatment in seniority-based layoff: "Some years ago there was a great concern with automating the procedures on the New York waterfront, and there was enormous hostility by the unions to any sort of automation because that was going to result in many job losses. But finally, when some program which was heavily subsidized by the Government was developed which provided compensation for those people affected by the automation, the program was carried forward."[26]

A Remedy for Racial Impact of Seniority-Based Advancement

Preferential treatment can also reduce the racist impact of seniority-based advancement. This AA strategy was used in a Kaiser plant in Gramercy, Louisiana, whose black population ratio was four times the black plant ratio. Black and white plant workers were racially grouped; each received 50 percent of the available craft training positions, which were then distributed by seniority within each racial group.[27] This preferential measure advanced some less senior blacks over more senior whites. Nevertheless, the Supreme Court endorsed Kaiser's program upgrading minority employees in *United Steelworkers of America* v. *Weber* (1979).[28]

In *Weber*, the court did not order compensation for the more senior whites who were held back by racial preference in advancement; however, in Chapter 4 I argue that these whites were entitled to compensation for their loss.

26. Statement by Howard Glickstein in *Last Hired, First Fired*, Informal Hearing before the United States Commission on Civil Rights, October 12, 1976 (Washington, D.C.: U.S. Commission on Civil Rights, 1976), p. 72.
27. See Ezorsky.
28. *United Steelworkers of America* v. *Weber* 443 U.S. 193 (1979).

Remedies for the Effects of
Departmental Seniority

As we have seen, departmental seniority arrangements were an obstacle for black workers who wished to transfer to a better, "white" department, because under such arrangements a transfer was stripped of all seniority credits. Hence blacks were locked into the "black" departments to which many had been assigned by racially biased supervisors.

The AA response was plantwide seniority. Under that system, workers could transfer without loss of accrued seniority. Thus a 1974 agreement reached by the U.S. government, nine major steel producers, and the United Steelworkers union agreed to calculate seniority by "length of service at each plant" rather than in a specific department.[29]

"Red-circling" was also introduced by some large auto producers to facilitate transfer. In certain situations, moving to a different department entails a pay cut, but where red-circling is practiced, the wages of the worker who transfers cannot be reduced. Hence the black worker who moves to a "white" department risks no pay loss.[30]

All racially preferential seniority remedies are specific since their implementation is based on explicit criteria of race and years of employment. They provide advantages for black workers only. But while plantwide seniority and work-sharing are also specific remedies because they are administered according to explicit criteria, these remedies are quasi-racial, because they also benefit some whites. Under plantwide seniority arrangements, whites who transfer to another department retain their seniority credits. Work-sharing benefits white, recently hired, usually younger workers who are vulnerable to seniority-based layoff.

29. "Steel Industry–E.E.O.C. Race and Sex Settlement," *Lab. Rel. Yearbook* (BNA) (1975): 371, 372.
30. See Gould, pp. 74, 374.

The Beneficial Impact of AA Programs

By the early 1980s, blacks had gained significantly from AA programs in employment. A dramatic increase in black employment and promotion occurred at specific companies that adopted affirmative action plans. These companies include AT&T, IBM, Levi-Strauss, and Sears Roebuck.[31]

AA programs also greatly improved minority representation in specific occupations and industries with poor records for black employment. In the steel industry, black workers made significant progress in obtaining skilled positions.[32] By 1982, in the Philadelphia area, where the famous Philadelpha Plan was instituted, minority employment in construction rose from one percent to 12 percent.[33] The large increase in black employment during the 1960s in South Carolina textiles, an industry that had virtually barred black workers, was due in large part to the activities of the EEOC and the Office of Federal Contract Compliance, which oversees the affirmative action obligations of companies holding government contracts.[34] Because cities have had a history of excluding blacks from employment, court rulings have required that blacks be hired as police officers and firefighters in many major cities. By 1982, 20,000 black officers had been added to police forces around the nation.[35]

As we have seen, Title 7 discrimination remedies were instrumental in effecting such AA measures as establishing numerical

---

31. *Affirmative Action to Open the Doors*, pp. 126–28.
32. W. L. Taylor, "*Brown*, Equal Protection, and the Isolation of the Poor," *Yale Law Journal* 95 (1986): 1713.
33. *Affirmative Action to Open the Doors*, p. 127.
34. *A Common Destiny: Blacks and American Society*, ed. Gerald David Jaynes and Robin M. Williams, Jr., for the Committee on the Status of Black Americans, Commission on Behavioral and Social Sciences and Education, National Research Council (Washington, D.C.: National Academy Press, 1989) p. 318.
35. *Affirmative Action to Open the Doors*, p. 128.

goals, recruitment of basically qualified blacks, and requiring job-related testing. *A Common Destiny* sums up the effect of such Title 7 remedies on the labor-market status of blacks:

> Title VII has had a tremendous effect on behavior in the U.S. labor market. . . . [Title VII] cases have produced dozens of important judicial rulings that changed the behavior of employers and unions toward blacks and other discriminated groups. . . . Major legal changes have occurred in seniority rules, hiring and promotion practices, and even in what constitutes labor market discrimination and have had wide-reaching [positive] effects on blacks' relative position in the labor market.

A Common Destiny also notes that enforcement of Executive Order 11246, which requires AA goals and timetables for government contractors, has produced "generally" positive results for blacks in employment.[36] Other beneficiaries of AA were black law and medical students, admitted under AA plans. As we shall see, contrary to critics, disadvantaged blacks have benefited significantly from AA programs, in professional schools as well as in employment.

After 1980: The Decline of AA

These AA remedies were primarily developed before 1980. After 1980 there was a dramatic decline in the enforcement of AA through the federal contract compliance program.[37] The effectiveness of AA also declined as a result of Supreme Court decisions during the 1980s.

36. *A Common Destiny*, pp. 319, 317.
37. Jonathan S. Leonard, "The Impact of Affirmative Action Regulation and Equal Employment Law on Black Employment," *Journal of Economic Perspectives* 4 (Fall 1990): 52.

The Supreme Court ruled against preference for retaining minorities in layoff in *Firefighters Local Union No. 1784 v. Stotts et al.* (1984). As a consequence, Federal District Court Judge Sarokin "reluctantly" withdrew his 1984 *Vulcan* court order, which had prescribed such preferential retention of minorities in seniority-based layoff, with compensation to adversely affected whites. Judge Sarokin asserted that "cities or states bent upon discriminatory practices" now could "continue to do so under the guide of economic reduction" and "women and minorities will be the first to go."[38]

As we have seen, the Supreme Court had ruled in *Griggs v. Duke Power Co.* (1971) that where qualification standards had disparate impact on minorities the employer must demonstrate that these standards served a "business necessity." Almost two decades later, however, the court weakened the business necessity requirement. In *Wards Cove* (1989), the court stated that such standards do not have to be essential to the employer's business.[39] The court also shifted the costly burden of proof for the significance of the challenged practice from the employer to the complainant.

AA was further weakened by the Supreme Court decision in *Martin v. Wilks* (1989). Court-approved settlements that established numerical goals and preferential treatment for minorities had long been regarded as immune from legal challenge. Now, as a consequence of this case, such settlements can later be challenged by white workers, who were not a party to the proceedings.[40]

During the same year, numerical set-asides for minority business contractors in Richmond were invalidated by the Supreme

38. Judge H. Lee Sarokin, quoted in "Judge Reverses Layoff Ruling on Minorities," *New York Times,* June 22, 1984.
39. *Wards Cove Packing Co. v. Atonio,* 109 S.Ct. 2115 (1989).
40. *Martin v. Wilks,* 109 S.Ct. 2180 (1989).

Court in *City of Richmond v. J. A. Croson Co.* (1989). Consequently, minority businesses have suffered substantial economic losses.[41]

41. *City of Richmond v. J. A. Croson Co.,* 109 S.Ct. 706 (1989); "Courts Are Undoing Efforts to Aid Minority Contractors," *New York Times,* July 16, 1990.

Part 2

Criticisms of Affirmative Action

3

Instrumental Criticism

In this chapter I appraise claims made by those who argue that AA is a poor instrument for ending racism because it is irrelevant or ineffective or even counterproductive. I analyze the claims of critics who raise moral objections to AA in Chapter 4.

Arguments against Statistical Representation

The ultimate goal of AA for blacks is occupational integration, that is, their approximate statistical representation in the hierarchy of employment as in the population at large. That goal was criticized by sociologists Daniel Bell and Nathan Glazer.

According to Bell, the logic of the claim for such racial representation implies that all groups—political conservatives, for example—should have balanced representation throughout employment.[1]

1. Daniel Bell, "On Meritocracy and Equality," *Public Interest*, February 1972:37–38.

Not so. Suppose both political conservatives and blacks are "underrepresented" on a university faculty. Surely the context of underrepresentation for each group is relevantly different. Because of the devastating impact of overt and institutional racism, blacks are disproportionately excluded from desirable employment and positions of power *throughout society.* No relevantly similar context exists for political conservatives. Hence while conservatives may be "underrepresented" in some pocket of employment, their situation is not analogous to the situation of blacks. I conclude that an AA commitment to parity in employment for blacks does not imply the same commitment for all groups.

Glazer claims that the goal of statistical representation of minorities in employment ignores "certain realities of community":

> Racial and ethnic communities have expressed themselves in occupations and work groups. Distinctive histories have channelled ethnic and racial groups into one kind of work or another, and this is the origin of many of the "unrepresentative" work distributions we see. These distributions have been maintained by an occupational tradition linked to an ethnic community which makes it easier for the Irish to become policemen, the Italians fruit dealers, Jews businessmen, and so on.[2]

It is true that tradition has channeled some groups into certain types of work. But while Glazer reminds us that because of historic tradition the Irish have become policemen, he fails to mention the "distinctive history" that has "channeled" blacks into the most miserable work, the distinctive history of two centuries of slavery and the murderous racism of the post-Reconstruction century. I suggest that black persons have not expressed themselves in such labor. Indeed, when offered opportunities by

2. Nathan Glazer, *Affirmative Discrimination* (New York: Basic Books, 1975), p. 203.

affirmative action programs, they were perfectly ready to express themselves in better jobs.

The Success of Other Minorities

Other minorities in the United States—European immigrants, for example—who have been victimized by discrimination moved up in American society without the assistance of AA measures. The success of other persecuted groups, such as the Jews, has suggested to some individuals that fault for the depressed status of blacks may lie not in racism but in themselves.[3] If this view is correct, the justification for AA appears questionable.

The situations of yesterday's European white immigrants and blacks are not analogous, however. Ethnic prejudice was not as virulent or pervasive as racism. White immigrants could assimilate while blacks were forced, in many states by law and the threat of lynching and in other states by unwritten law, to remain segregated from white society. Indeed, overt racism contributed to the occupational ascent of newly arrived whites. For many such whites eviction of a black worker from a job was the beginning of upward mobility. Thus white immigrants drove black employees out of railroads, streetcars, construction, and shipbuilding. The influx of whites into Birmingham's mills destroyed the concentration of blacks in a number of trades. When New York City's European immigrant population reached 76 percent of the total population, eviction of blacks was intensified.

3. "Jews have moved up in American life by utilizing middle-class skills—reason, orderliness, conservation of capital, and a high valuation and use of education. . . . Finding that playing by 'the rules of the game'—reward based on merit, training and seniority—has worked for them, many Jews wonder why Negroes do not utilize the same methods for getting ahead." Murray Friedman describes this view without endorsing it in "The Jews," in *Through Different Eyes*, ed. Peter I. Rose et al. (New York: Oxford University Press, 1973), pp. 52–53.

They were steadily pushed out of their jobs as wagon and coach drivers, house painters, tailors, longshore workers, brick layers, and waiters.[4]

According to sociologist Robert Blauner, Jewish, Irish, Italian, and German immigrants benefited from racism. For example, decent jobs were usurped from northern blacks by incoming Germans, Irish, and Italians, and as a consequence these black workers were driven into the marginal reaches of the economy. He concludes: "Without such a combination of immigration and white racism, the Harlems and the South Chicagos might have become solid working class and middle-class communities with the economic and social resources to absorb and aid the incoming masses of [black] Southerners, much as the European ethnic groups have been able to do for their newcomers."[5]

Also, the attitude of trade unions toward white immigrants and blacks differed sharply. In the early twentieth century, trade unions contributed to the impoverishment of black people either by excluding them, as did the craft unions, or, like the powerful International Ladies' Garment Workers Union, by cooperating in their segregation into the lowest-paid employment. On the other hand, European immigrants established an "ethnic lock" on types of employment or on craft-union jurisdiction. Thus in New York there was a Greek furriers' local, an Italian dressmakers' union, a Jewish waiters' organization, and so forth.[6]

Thomas Sowell claims that recent immigrants who became racial minorities in the United States—such as the Asians and West Indians—are significantly more successful than native blacks and rival whites in achievement.[7] However, many of these recent

4. Herbert Hill, "Race, Ethnicity, and Organized Labor: The Opposition to Affirmative Action," *New Politics* 1, n.s. (1987): 45–52.

5. Robert Blauner, *Racial Oppression in America* (New York: Harper and Row, 1972), p. 64.

6. Hill, pp. 51–52.

7. Thomas Sowell, *Civil Rights: Rhetoric or Reality?* (New York: Quill, William Morrow, 1984), esp. pp. 77 and 130–31.

arrivals have an initial advantage over native blacks. International migration from third-world countries to the United States is highly selective, bringing in skilled, educated persons, among whom are scientists, engineers, doctors, and academics. Such selectivity has created an international "brain drain."[8] Such immigrants are likely to set high economic goals for themselves because they arrive with economic and social-class advantages, such as substantial capital, as well as occupational and business experience.[9] According to a study of Koreans in New York City, the advantage of class resources attained in their homeland—higher education, professional experience, economic motivation, and money—provided "decisive" support for their success in small business. The Korean case is only one example of the importance of social-class origins for such success.[10]

Although Asian immigrants have been drawn disproportionately from occupational elites, the more recent immigrants among them include a large number of unskilled and uneducated workers, whose lives provide a sharp contrast to the Asian success story. In Chinatown, they labor long hours in restaurants and sweatshops for miserable wages, without hope of advancement. For these "Downtown Chinese," crime—break-ins, drug trafficking, and street shootouts by armed teenagers—ranks as one of their most serious problems.[11]

It is true that West Indian black immigrants have been more successful occupationally than African Americans. The virtual absence of a white working class in the West Indian homeland, where blacks held majority status, facilitated their acquisition of

8. Thomas D. Boston, *Race, Class, and Conservatism* (Boston: Unwin Hyman, 1988), p. 88.

9. Nancy Foner, "New Immigrants and Changing Patterns in New York City," in *New Immigrants in New York,* ed. Nancy Foner (New York: Columbia University Press, 1987), pp. 14–15.

10. Foner, pp. 14–15.

11. Peter Kwong, *The New Chinatown* (New York: Noonday Press, Farrar, Straus, and Giroux, 1987), pp. 5–7, 120–24.

skilled trades. According to a study of U.S. immigration records in the 1920s, West Indians had advantages in literacy and skills, advantages that are conducive to an achievement orientation and that would tend to be replicated in their children. Although later West Indian migrants were more occupationally diverse, they benefited from this preexisting community, which provided patronage for West Indian professionals and entrepreneurs.[12]

Such advantages have contributed to the greater ability of West Indians, by comparison with African Americans, to meet the race-neutral qualification standards of employers and to ascend the occupational ladder. An analysis of the Census of 1980, however, does not corroborate the view that West Indian economic achievement rivals that of whites. According to that analysis, family income and male earnings of blacks of West Indian ancestry are significantly inferior to whites. In New York City a native white male college graduate can expect to earn 50 percent more than an equally educated black male of West Indian ancestry. In the South a native white male high-school graduate can expect to earn 60 percent more than an equally educated black of West Indian descent.[13]

In her introduction to a collection of 1987 studies of black immigrants in New York City, Nancy Foner points out that West Indians are "stigmatized as blacks." "Used to societies where blacks were a majority and where education, income and culture partially 'erased' one's blackness, West Indians find that their skin color now brands them as inferior to the white majority and that they face racial discrimination in housing, employment and innumerable personal encounters."[14]

12. Stephen Steinberg, *The Ethnic Myth: Race, Ethnicity, and Class in America,* updated and expanded ed. (Boston: Beacon Press, 1989), pp. 275–79.

13. Reynolds Farley, "West Indian Success: Myth or Fact?" (unpublished manuscript, Ann Arbor, Mich.: Population Studies Center, University of Michigan, 1987).

14. Foner, "New Immigrants," p. 11.

Does Preference Reinforce White Prejudice?

Some AA plans permit hiring a "basically qualified" black rather than a better qualified white. According to sociologist Christopher Jencks, such preference reinforces white prejudice about black incompetence.[15]

But white prejudice tends to be exacerbated not only by racial preference but also by those impartial equal-opportunity measures which move some blacks ahead of whites for well-paid positions of status and authority over whites. Catering to such bias may in some cases require the demise not merely of preference but of equal-opportunity rules.

Moreover, prejudiced whites are biased in their perception of black competence. In some situations evaluation cannot exclude subjective factors (for example, a qualitative appraisal of scholarship). In such cases, biased whites tend to underrate the performance of blacks. Hence, where blacks are equally or slightly more qualified than their white competitors, prejudiced whites will tend to perceive these blacks as comparatively less qualified. These whites will construe employment of these blacks based on racial impartiality as racial preference to inferior candidates. Should these black candidates be denied equal opportunity because its consequences reinforce the prejudice of biased whites?

Some persons believe that advocacy of preference instead of mere equal opportunity assumes inherent black inferiority. But the appropriate response to such individuals is to demonstrate that preference is necessary not because of black inferiority but because the handicap of a segregated racist past has robbed many blacks of the wherewithal to compete equally with whites.

AA programs do not require employers to hire unqualified

15. Christopher Jencks, *New York Review of Books*, March 17, 1983: 14.

blacks. On the contrary, a "basically qualified" employee is competent to do the job. Indeed, in some cases these blacks may be superior to workers hired by traditional preference (e.g., to relatives).

Moreover, the stereotype that worries Jencks is exemplified by a black who as a consequence of such preference is employed. There is a different stereotype, the unemployed black—lazy or a welfare cheat—which is far more significant.

A 1990 survey showed that a majority of Americans see blacks in a "decidedly negative light" on such characteristics as laziness and a preference for living on welfare. Midge Decter, a political writer, states that the idea that the "hordes" of male youth on ghetto street corners ever really looked for a job is simply "laughable." And according to Ronnie Dugger, editor of the *Texas Observer*, Ronald Reagan told a Florida audience in 1976, that working people at grocery check-out counters were outraged when a "strapping young buck" bought T-bone steaks with food stamps. Dugger ironically concluded: "It was out in the open . . . the welfare cheat was black."[16]

This view of black persons as unwilling to work is sustained by their relatively higher joblessness; however, effective enforcement of such AA measures as numerical hiring goals which move employers to hire and train basically qualified and "qualifiable" blacks can reduce black unemployment.

The relevance of such AA measures for jobless high-school teenagers from welfare or below-poverty-level families is indicated by this 1984 report of a subsidized work and training program:

16. Tom W. Smith, *Ethnic Images*, GSS Topical Report No. 19 (National Opinion Research Center, University of Chicago, 1990), p. 8; Midge Decter, "Looting and Liberal Racism," *Commentary* 64 (1977): 51; Ronnie Dugger, *On Reagan, the Man and His Presidency* (New York: McGraw-Hill, 1983), pp. 200–201.

Instrumental Criticism

When the jobs are available minority [high-school] youths want to work, even at the minimum wage and while continuing school. . . . Given some quality work experience . . . their chances of labor market success are substantially improved.[17]

A 1980 study of a work-training program for welfare mothers states:

Many of the [welfare mothers] . . . sought and obtained jobs and remained employed even though their earnings were substantially offset by loss of welfare benefits. Many female heads of household are willing to work for very small financial gains in preference to the social opprobrium of continuing on welfare and suffering the governmental interference in their lives associated with being on public assistance.[18]

Also, black overrepresentation among job losers—many of whom become "discouraged" workers who drop out of the work force—can be reduced by AA measures such as work-sharing and seniority preference.

Has AA Helped Only Advantaged Blacks?

According to some critics, AA benefits only "a few fortunate" blacks.[19] On the contrary, among men, AA has increased the demand for "lowly educated" blacks as well as the more highly

17. *Post-Program Impacts of the Youth Incentive Entitlement Pilot Projects* (New York: Manpower Demonstration Research Corporation, 1984), pp. vi–viii.

18. *Summary and Findings of the Nationally Supported Work Demonstration,* Manpower Demonstration Research Corporation (Cambridge, Mass.: Ballinger, 1980), p. 6.

19. See, for example, Carl Cohen, "What Is 'Affirmative Action'?" *Texas Law Review* 58 (1980): 859.

educated.[20] Moreover, AA enforcement has moved blacks up, not only into management, white-collar, and professional positions but also into semiskilled, service, blue-collar, craft, police, and firefighter jobs. In a 1986 *Yale Law Journal* article, legal scholar William L. Taylor summarizes these consequences of AA. He concludes:

> Although one criticism of affirmative action remedies has been that they tend to benefit minorities who are already advantaged or middle class, the results . . . suggest otherwise. The focus of much of the effort has been not just on white collar jobs, but also . . . on areas in which the extension of new opportunities has provided upward mobility for less advantaged minority workers. Nor does the criticism appear valid for the professions. Studies show that of the increased enrollment of minority students in medical schools during the 1970's, significant numbers were from families of low income and job status, indicating that the rising enrollment of minorities in professional schools stemming from affirmative action policies reflects increased mobility, not simply changing occupational preferences among middle class minority families.[21]

The southern textile industry provides an example of the benefits AA has brought to a severely disadvantaged black group. In the middle and late 1960s, government pressure for hiring blacks, exerted in a tight labor market, contributed to the dramatic improvement in the employment of black women in southern textile mills. Although previously excluded almost entirely from the mills, they were hired as laborers, operatives, and ser-

20. Jonathan S. Leonard, "Splitting Blacks?: Affirmative Action and Earnings Inequality within and across Races," *Proceedings of the Thirty-Ninth Annual Meeting,* Industrial Relations Research Association Series, ed. Barbara D. Dennis (1986), p. 57.
21. William L. Taylor, "*Brown,* Equal Protection, and the Isolation of the Poor," *Yale Law Journal* 95 (1986): 1713–14.

vice and craft workers.[22] As a result, these black women—many of whom had spent their working lives cleaning other people's homes for a few dollars a day—tripled their wages,—an enormous improvement in the quality of their lives.

I conclude that AA has not merely helped a "few fortunate" blacks.

AA and the Black "Underclass"

William J. Wilson, well-known analyst of disadvantaged blacks, indicates that AA programs should not be abandoned, but on the other hand he writes (in a *New York Times* 1989 op-ed as a policy recommendation to the Democratic party) "Many white Americans have turned not against blacks but against a strategy that emphasizes programs perceived to benefit only minorities." He advocates "universal policies," such as full employment and health care, which are "race-blind," rather than AA programs, which are race-conscious.[23] That is the thesis I criticize here.

In his book *The Truly Disadvantaged* (1987), Wilson grants that some disadvantaged blacks have benefited from AA, but not the *truly* disadvantaged, the ghetto "underclass." Wilson describes this group as "outside the mainstream of the American occupational system. Included in this group are individuals who lack training and skills and either experience long-term unemployment or are not members of the labor force, individuals who are engaged in street crime and other forms of aberrant behavior,

22. Richard L. Rowan, "The Negro in the Textile Industry," in Herbert R. Northrup, Richard L. Rowan, et al., *Negro Employment in Southern Industry: A Study of Racial Policies in Five Industries*, Studies of Negro Employment 4 (Philadelphia: University of Pennsylvania Press, 1970).

23. William J. Wilson, *New York Times*, op-ed, March 24, 1989.

and families that experience long-term spells of poverty and/or welfare dependency. These are the populations to which I refer when I speak of the *underclass*" (emphasis in original). To benefit these blacks, Wilson advocates a macroeconomic policy designed to promote economic growth and employment with on-the-job training[24] (hereafter the Expansion Proposal).

Let us look more closely at the truly disadvantaged blacks, who, according to Wilson, have not benefited from AA. It is important to distinguish two kinds of persons who appear "outside the mainstream of the American occupational system": those who are so destroyed as persons as to be unemployable and untrainable and those who are motivated for work and training—if they have access to employment.

It is true that AA cannot help the first group in their present situation, but neither can Wilson's Expansion Proposal. Increased employment opportunities cannot help individuals who are unable to work, so such programs could not be more effective than AA in helping these disadvantaged persons. Neither strategy can eliminate the need for drug rehabilitation programs, better schools, and other social programs.

The second group includes unemployed welfare mothers and youth. As we have seen, however, studies of supported work and training programs for women and minority youths (high-school teenagers from welfare or below-poverty-level families) showed that a significant number were seriously motivated for employment. The second group also includes numerous formerly employed blacks whose employment history indicates they are capable of work. These include blacks who lost their jobs in seniority-based layoffs, as well as a large number whose positions were wiped out by structural economic changes, such as the decline in manufacture where blacks were disproportionately

24. William J. Wilson, *The Truly Disadvantaged* (Chicago: University of Chicago Press, 1987), pp. 8, 151.

employed as blue-collar workers. In 1984, 52 percent of unemployed blacks had been displaced from the jobs at which they were working.[25] Significant numbers of blacks, impoverished high-school youths, welfare mothers, and displaced workers, many of whom are members of the group that Wilson describes as "underclass," are therefore in fact capable of working.

Wilson suggests, however, that AA cannot rectify the mismatch between the skill and education demands of today's high-tech economy and the surplus of comparatively less educated and untrained blacks, among whom are blue-collar workers, unemployed because of the decline in manufacturing. Again, Wilson's criticism of the inappropriateness of AA would apply equally well to his Expansion Proposal. Increasing the number of jobs will not give employment to blacks who because of inadequate education are incapable of performing them.

The relevant fact is that, while a number of large cities have lost manufacturing jobs, many have gained a greater number of positions. Of the 15 million net jobs created in the past decade, the majority are in the service industries. Among the new workers are restaurant employees, bank and retail clerks, hotel maids, computer assemblers, health-care personnel, fast-food workers, and others laboring in wholesale warehouses on inventories, at supermarket check-out counters, and in the back offices of financial firms. Although many of these job holders identify themselves as "white collar," they, like their blue-collar predecessors on the assembly line, toil at repetitive, routinized tasks.[26]

Moreover, the authors of *A Common Destiny* (1989) inform us that the importance of social networks for access to employ-

25. U.S. Department of Labor, Bureau of Labor Statistics, *Employment and Earnings* 32 (January 1985): 167; cited in Billy J. Tidwell, "A Profile of the Black Unemployed," in *The State of Black America* (New York: National Urban League, 1987), p. 226.

26. William Serrin, "A Great American Job Machine?" *Nation*, September 18, 1989: 269–72.

ment—especially in service industries—has probably increased. Because black youths live in a racially segregated society, they have social ties primarily to black neighbors, school friends, and relatives and are outside the "principal" (white) employment networks: "Older black males—concentrated in blue-collar jobs in now-declining manufacturing industries—are of little help to young blacks seeking jobs in service industries today."[27] Black youths, lacking the right connections to whites, are deprived of opportunities for service-sector employment. As I described earlier, an effective AA remedy for reducing the racist impact of a white pipeline to jobs is minority outreach, strengthened by numerical goals and timetables, with preference to basically qualified blacks.

Economic changes that have moved jobs from the city to distant white suburbs are an important factor in creating black unemployment.[28] Among these newly created suburban jobs, inaccessible by public transportation from inner cities, are positions as secretaries, retail sales clerks, nurses' aides, bookkeepers, cooks, and cashiers.[29] However, guidelines to Executive Order 11246 for developing affirmative action programs recommend that where lack of transportation inhibits minority employment it is appropriate for companies to take special corrective action.[30] Black youths isolated in ghettos sustained by decades of

27. *A Common Destiny: Blacks and American Society,* ed. Gerald David Jaynes and Robin M. Williams, Jr., for the Committee on the Status of Black Americans, Commission on Behavioral and Social Sciences and Education, National Research Council (Washington, D.C.: National Academy Press, 1989), p. 321.

28. "Urban Jobless Joined to Suburban Jobs," *New York Times,* October 25, 1989.

29. Committee on Policy for Racial Justice, *Visions of a Better Way* (Washington, D.C.: Joint Center for Political Studies Press, 1989), pp. 15–16.

30. U.S. Department of Labor, Office of Federal Contract Compliance, Code of Federal Regulations, 60-2-23 (b), *Federal Register* 36 (December 4, 1971).

racism could ride "Equal Opportunity" buses to white suburbs where decent jobs awaited them.

AA can also help blacks who are excluded from service-industry jobs by higher education requirements. We have seen that although many blacks who attended ghetto schools cannot meet the relevant job or training requirements of employers, employers have often exaggerated their educational requirements at the expense of blacks, or even for the purpose of excluding them. Indeed, Wilson grants that many positions, "identified as 'higher education' jobs . . . may not really require 'higher educational' training."[31] Where these requirements are invalid, not essential to job performance, insistence on the AA *Griggs* remedy is a relevant countermeasure (and would be more effective if its teeth were restored).

Moreover, as indicated earlier, company training programs can help reduce the effect of educational handicaps. Also, requirements such as probationary employment periods and sophisticated candidate screening can effectively test for work habits that employers associate with a college diploma.

Undeniably, increased education will strengthen the position of blacks in the labor market. But generally speaking, by keeping the employment door wide open for blacks, AA increases their incentive to acquire more education. It is well documented that the perceived life chances of low-income students reduce their scholastic motivation.[32] But increased education alone will not do the trick. Blacks who have been better matched than whites for some positions that require higher education have suffered greater unemployment. In 1980 blacks with college educations had a higher unemployment rate than did white high-school dropouts.[33]

31. Wilson, *The Truly Disadvantaged*, p. 102.
32. *Visions of a Better Way*, p. 15.
33. "I Feel So Helpless," *Time*, June 16, 1980: 21.

While Wilson does not propose that AA programs be eliminated, for the most part he ignores AA's record of success. As we have seen, *A Common Destiny* reports, first, the generally positive effect of Executive Order 11246, which requires AA programs for government contractors and, second, the "tremendous impact" of Title 7 on the position of blacks in the labor market (see Chapter 2, above). The authors single out the AT&T agreement as exemplifying the beneficial results of court-ordered decrees.[34] The Philadelphia Plan, the *Weber* case, the *Griggs* decision, and the Steel Industry Settlement also serve as landmarks of successful affirmative action.

The issue is not merely jobs for blacks, but opportunities for moving up. Traditionally blacks have been concentrated in government jobs not merely because such positions were more accessible but because chances for promotion in the private sector were far fewer. Where AA has been enforced, however, blacks have made significant progress at all levels of employment. Indeed, according to economist Jonathan Leonard, much of AA's "positive impact on minority wages . . . has been due to promotions within broad occupational categories."[35]

Wilson's emphasis on proposing race-blind programs for full employment and economic growth, rather than AA, suggests that we have a choice: either AA or such programs. That conception of the issue is misleading. It would be unreasonable to advocate AA as a substitute for these economic policies. But the relevant fact is that in periods of economic growth AA's importance would be quite significant.

Although in an expanding economy more on-the-job training opportunities exist, the record shows that without enforcement of AA training goals blacks are often excluded from such opportunities. As we have seen, the allocation of training positions to

34. *A Common Destiny*, p. 319.
35. Leonard, "Splitting Blacks?" p. 53.

incumbent workers by race-neutral seniority often tends to exclude blacks. However, that racist impact is reduced by AA programs requiring preferential seniority selection for training, such as the program upheld by the Supreme Court in *Weber*. Construction unions have persistently denied training apprenticeships to young black applicants, and recent history has demonstrated that without strong enforcement of AA goals and timetables such white-dominated unions will continue to distribute these well-paid apprenticeships to their white friends and relatives. Even in periods of economic expansion, blacks have been "last hired." Granted that because the number of openings increases during such periods, employers reach down to the back of the queue for these "last hired," so that blacks undoubtedly benefit when the number of jobs increases. This benefit to blacks is the rationale of Wilson's Expansion Proposal; however, I suggest that to adopt that strategy as a *substitute* for AA is ill advised.

Consider this analogy: Before bus desegregation, blacks could occupy only a relatively small number of seats in the back of the bus; hence they often had to stand. If there were more buses, blacks would have gained more seats, but Wilson certainly would not have advocated building more buses as a substitute for desegregation, that is, as a substitute for racial justice. Let us then not conceive of expansion in the number of jobs as a substitute for racial justice in the workplace.

The situation of blacks in the workplace without AA is not difficult to imagine. The racist impact of irrelevant job requirements will continue, perpetuating the victimizing effects of inferior ghetto education and the racial bias that has denied blacks training and work experience. Unless AA measures reduce the racist impact of seniority-based layoff, blacks will, as always, move down during recessions into unemployment. Should blacks wait until recessions are eliminated (until capitalism is fundamentally restructured) to achieve job security? Without AA, desirable jobs will be distributed through a white pipeline, an ingrained practice in America's two segregated societies. Occupational segregation has always meant that blacks as a group are situated at the bottom of employment. The better, decent-paying jobs are largely a white preserve. The aim of AA is to break that racist barrier. Without that pressure, even in an expanding economy, occupational segregation will continue. Blacks will remain second-class citizens.

Finally, Wilson believes that AA is politically implausible: because it is designed to benefit racial minorities, AA lacks wide appeal.[36] But in fact AA programs in education, hiring, training, and promotion benefit not only blacks but other minorities and women, who are over 50 percent of the population. The groups that benefit from AA measures constitute the overwhelming majority of the nation.

36. Wilson, *New York Times*, op-ed, March 24, 1989.

4

Moral Perspectives on Affirmative Action

AA's benefits to blacks can be viewed from both a forward-looking and a backward-looking moral perspective.[1] From a forward-looking perspective, the purpose of AA is to reduce institutional racism, thereby moving blacks toward the goal of occupational integration. When that goal is achieved, millions of blacks will no longer be unfairly barred by the effects of their racist history from employment benefits. Moreover, such integration will significantly dissipate invidious racist attitudes. As I have suggested earlier, individuals socialized in a world where blacks are assimilated throughout the hierarchy of employment will no longer readily assume that they belong at the bottom.

From a backward-looking perspective, blacks have a moral claim to compensation for past injury. The paramount injustice perpetrated against blacks—enslavement—requires such com-

1. For moral justifications of AA-type benefits to blacks which are also both backward and forward looking but differ in some respects from mine, see Howard McGary, Jr., "Justice and Reparations," *Philosophical Forum* 9 (1977–78): 250–63; Bernard R. Boxill, *Blacks and Social Justice* (Totowa, N.J.: Rowman and Allanheld, 1984), chap. 7.

pensation. If the effects of that murderous institution had been dissipated over time, the claim to compensation now would certainly be weaker. From the post-Reconstruction period to the present, however, racist practices have continued to transmit and reinforce the consequences of slavery. Today blacks still predominate in those occupations that in a slave society would be reserved for slaves.

Such ongoing racism has not been the work only of private parties. The racism of government practices encouraged race discrimination by landlords who blocked the escape of blacks from ghettos, and by employers and unions who refused to hire, promote, or train them, as well as widespread communication of an insulting stereotype of blacks, derogatory to their ability and character. During the first two-thirds of this century, racism was in many respects official public policy. That policy included: legally compulsory segregation into inferior private and publicly owned facilities such as schools, which—as recognized in *Brown v. Board of Education of Topeka* (1954)—violated the constitutional rights of black children; court-upheld racially restrictive covenants in the transfer of private residences; antimiscegenation laws that resembled the prohibition of marriage by persons with venereal diseases; race discrimination in government practices such as public employment, voting registration procedures, federal assistance to business persons and farmers, and allocation of state and municipal services to black neighborhoods (e.g., police protection, sanitation, and educational resources); manifest racial bias in the courts; and pervasive police brutality against black people.

The practices of the Federal Housing Authority exemplified governmental racism. For decades after its inception in 1934, the FHA, which insured mortgage loans, enshrined racial segregation as public policy. The agency set itself up as the protector of all-white neighborhoods, especially in the suburbs. According to urban planner Charles Abrams, the FHA's racial policies could "well have been culled from the Nuremberg Laws."[2] Today white suburban youths continue to benefit from the past racist practices of this government agency. Not only will they inherit homes purchased with the FHA assistance, denied to blacks; they also enjoy racially privileged access to the expanding employment opportunities in all-white suburbs. In 1973, legal scholar Boris I. Bittker summed up governmental misconduct against blacks: "More than any other form of official misconduct, racial discrimination against blacks was systematic, unrelenting, authorized at the highest governmental levels, and practiced by large segments of the population."[3] The role of government in practicing, protecting, and providing sanction for racism by private parties suffices to demonstrate the moral legitimacy of legally required compensation to blacks.

This past of pervasive racism—public and private—follows blacks into the labor market, as we have seen. They are also especially vulnerable to recessionary layoffs because they possess far smaller reserves of money and property to sustain them during periods of joblessness. Such vulnerability also affects many newly middle-class blacks who, lacking inherited or accumulated assets, are—as the saying goes—two paychecks away from poverty.

Are AA measures, such as preferential treatment in employment, an appropriate method of compensation for blacks? In

2. Quoted in Kenneth T. Jackson, *Crabgrass Frontier* (New York: Oxford University Press, 1985), p. 214.

3. Boris I. Bittker, *The Case for Black Reparations* (New York: Random House, 1973), p. 21. The summary of past injustices to blacks is based on Bittker, chap. 2; Michael Reich, "The Economics of Racism," *The Capitalist System*, ed. Richard C. Edwards, Michael Reich, and Thomas E. Weisskopf (Englewood Cliffs, N.J.: Prentice-Hall, 1972); Jackson, pp. 213–14; *A Common Destiny: Blacks and American Society*, ed. Gerald David Jaynes and Robin M. Williams, Jr., for the Committee on the Status of Black Americans, Commission on Behavioral and Social Sciences and Education, National Research Council (Washington, D.C.: National Academy Press, 1989), p. 366.

fact, federal and state governments recognized the appropriateness of employment preference as an instrument of compensation to veterans long before the adoption of AA measures.[4] This court-sanctioned policy has affected the employment of millions of workers, and in some states where veteran preference is practiced, nonveterans have practically no chance to obtain the best positions.

What are the specific claims of those who find moral fault with such programs? First, concerning the compensatory rationale for AA, some analysts argue that compensation for blacks is counterproductive. Others claim that better-off blacks do not deserve the compensation of preferential treatment, especially where whites excluded by such preference are themselves disadvantaged. Second, AA trammels the rights of others—of employers who have a right to hire whomever they please, or of white candidates who are wrongfully excluded by preferential treatment. Finally, some critics suggest that blacks themselves may be morally injured by racial preference, which allegedly damages their self-respect.

Compensation as Counterproductive?

Shelby Steele, a professor of English, criticizes the compensatory claim for AA, according to which AA is "something 'owed,' as reparation": "Suffering can be endured and overcome, it cannot be repaid. To think otherwise is to prolong the suffering."[5] But if compensation should be withheld from blacks because suffering cannot be repaid, then for the same reason compensation should also be withheld from veterans, Holocaust survivors, and victims of industrial accidents. Members of these groups do

4. Robert Fullinwinder, "The Equal Opportunity Myth," in *Report from the Center for Philosophy and Public Policy* (College Park: University of Maryland, Fall, 1981).

5. Shelby Steele, "A Negative Vote on Affirmative Action," *New York Times Magazine*, May 13, 1990.

not complain that compensation prolongs their "suffering"; on the contrary, they have often insisted on their right to such benefits. I see no reason for assuming that compensation per se injures its recipients.

Affluent Blacks as Undeserving

The philosopher William Blackstone criticizes the compensatory rationale for preferential treatment for affluent blacks:

> There is no invariable connection between a person's being black . . . and suffering from past invidious discrimination. . . . There are many blacks and other minority group members who are highly advantaged, who are sons and daughters of well-educated, affluent lawyers, doctors and industrialists. A policy of reverse discrimination would mean that such highly advantaged individuals would receive preferential treatment over the sons and daughters of disadvantaged whites or disadvantaged members of other minorities. I submit that such a situation is not social justice.[6]

Blackstone offers two arguments: (1) Black persons born into better-off black families have not suffered discrimination; hence, he suggests, they do not deserve compensation. (2) Preference that benefits these blacks at the expense of disadvantaged non-blacks is unjust.

First, it is false that blacks born into better-off families have not been injured by discrimination. Because racist treatment of blacks in business and professions reduced family income, it hurt their sons and daughters. Among the racist injuries these black parents suffered were the racially discriminatory policies of fed-

---

6. William T. Blackstone, "Reverse Discrimination and Compensatory Justice," in *Social Justice and Preferential Treatment*, ed. William T. Blackstone and Robert T. Heslep (Athens: University of Georgia Press, 1977), p. 67.

eral agencies in allocation of business loans, low-interest mortgages, agrarian price supports, and government contracts.[7] They also were victimized by racist exclusion from practice in white law firms and hospitals and by legally imposed or encouraged residential and school segregation that impaired their education and isolated them from white business contacts. Because of such invidious discrimination, black professionals and entrepreneurs could do far less for their children than their white counterparts. Moreover, the sons and daughters of black lawyers, doctors, and business persons have themselves suffered the experience of living in a segregated, pervasively racist society.

Laurence Thomas, a black university professor of philosophy, attests to the humiliating distrust that he and other well-placed black academics endure today in public places.[8] Fears that affect blacks of all classes are described by Don Jackson, a black police sergeant who, while investigating reports of police racism in 1989, was stopped by white police officers, one of whom shoved Jackson's head through a window during the arrest.

> The feeling that no matter how hard you worked you could always be reduced to the status of a "field nigger" haunts the lives of black Americans at every economic stratum. . . . It has long been the role of the police to see that the plantation mentality is passed from one generation of blacks to another. . . . The black American finds that the most prominent reminder of his second-class citizenship are the police. . . . A variety of stringent laws were enacted and enforced to stamp the imprint of inequality on the mind of the black American. . . . No one has enforced these rules with more zeal than the police. Operating free of constitutional limitations, the police have long been the greatest nemesis of blacks, irrespective of whether they are complying with the law or not. We have learned that there are cars we are not supposed to drive, streets we are not supposed to walk. We may still be

7. Bittker, pp. 16–17.
8. Laurence Thomas, *New York Times,* op-ed, August 13, 1990.

stopped and asked "Where are you going, boy?" Whether we're in a Mercedes or a Volkswagon.[9]

Even if one assumes that the economically better-off blacks are less deserving of compensation, it hardly follows that they do not deserve any compensation. As Bernard Boxill observes in *Blacks and Social Justice:* "Because I have lost only one leg, I may be less deserving of compensation than another who has lost two legs, but it does not follow that I deserve no compensation."[10]

It is true that where preference has been extended to blacks— as with craft workers, professionals, blue- and white-collar employees, teachers, police, and firefighters—some excluded whites may be financially less well off than the blacks who gained. This shift fails to show that these blacks were not victimized by invidious discrimination for which they should be compensated. Also, compensatory employment preference is sometimes given to veterans who are more affluent than the nonveterans who are thereby excluded from jobs. Indeed, some veterans gained, on the whole, from military life: placed in noncombat units, they often learned a valuable skill. Yet no one proposes that for this reason veteran preference be abandoned.

Unqualified Blacks as Unaffected by AA

Thomas Nagel, a philosopher who endorses preferential treatment, nevertheless faults the compensatory justification for such preference, claiming that blacks who benefit from it are probably not the ones who suffered most from discrimination; "those who don't have the qualifications even to be considered" do not gain from preferential policies.[11]

9. Don Jackson, *New York Times*, op-ed, January 23, 1989.
10. Boxill, p. 148.
11. Thomas Nagel, "A Defense of Affirmative Action," in *Report from the Center for Philosophy and Public Policy*, p. 7.

Of course, AA preference does not help blacks obtain very desirable employment if they lack the qualifications even to be considered for such positions. But preferential treatment in diverse areas of the public and private sector has benefited not only highly skilled persons but also poorly educated workers. It is also true that blacks who lack the qualifications even to be considered for *any* employment will not gain from AA preference. As I indicated in my critique of William J. Wilson, AA cannot help those so destroyed as to be incapable of any work or on-the-job training, who require other compensatory race-specific rehabilitation programs. But AA employment programs should not perform the function of these programs.[12] The claim that unemployable blacks are most deserving does not imply that employable blacks fail to deserve any—or even a great deal of—compensation.

Granted, we do not know whether the particular blacks who benefit from preference at each level in the hierarchy of employment are the very same individuals who, absent a racist past, would have qualified at that level by customary standards. Justified group compensation, however, does not require satisfaction of such rigid criteria. Veterans who enjoy hiring, promotion, and seniority preference are surely not the very same individuals who, absent their military service, would have qualified for the positions they gained by such preference.

Unlike job preference for veterans, AA racial preference in employment contributes to eradication of a future evil. It is an instrument for ending occupational segregation of blacks, a legacy of their enslavement.

The Rights of Employers

According to libertarian philosophers, laws that require any type of AA in the workplace—indeed, those merely requiring

12. Nor should AA employment programs substitute for other compensatory programs to blacks, such as cash payments to the elderly, compensatory educa-

passive nondiscrimination—violate the rights of private employers. The philosopher Robert Nozick suggests that the right of employers to hire is relevantly similar to the right of individuals to marry.[13] Just as individuals should be free to marry whomever they please, so private entrepreneurs should be free to employ whomever they please, and government should not interfere with employers in their hiring decisions.

But surely the freedom to choose one's spouse and the freedom to select one's employees are relevantly different. Individuals denied such freedom of choice in marriage are forced to give their bodies to their spouses. They are subject to rape—a destructive, brutal, and degrading intrusion. Marital choices belong to the deeply personal sphere where indeed government should keep out. State intervention in employment is another matter. To require that an auto plant hire some black machinists falls outside the sphere of the deeply personal; it is not, like rape, a destructive, brutal, and degrading personal intrusion. I conclude that the analogy between freedom to marry and freedom to hire fails.[14]

The Rights of White Candidates

According to some philosophers, while the social goal of preferential treatment may be desirable, the moral cost is too high.

---

tion programs in primary and secondary ghetto schools, and preferential admissions with effective financial support to black students for college and professional schools.

13. "If the woman who later became my wife rejected another suitor . . . would the rejected less intelligent and less handsome suitor have a legitimate complaint about unfairness . . . (Against whom would the rejected suitor have a legitimate complaint? Against what?). . . . The major objection to speaking of everyone's having a right *to* various things such as *equality of opportunity*, life and so on, and enforcing this right, is that these 'rights' require a substructure of things and materials and actions; and *other* people may have rights and entitlements over these" (Robert Nozick, *Anarchy, State, and Utopia* [New York: Basic Books, 1974], pp. 237–38; first and third emphases in original, second added).

14. Libertarians deny the right of government to interfere with private employers not only in hiring but also in determining working conditions, as by

The burden it imposes on adversely affected whites violates their right to equal treatment. They are unfairly singled out for sacrifice. Thomas Nagel states that "the most important argument against preferential treatment is that it subordinates the individual's right to equal treatment to broader social aims".[15]

Some proponents of preferential treatment reject the charge of unfairness because, as they see the matter, whites have either been responsible for immoral racist practices or have gained from them. According to this claim, all whites *deserve* to pay the cost of preferential treatment (hereafter, the desert claim).[16] I do not accept the desert claim; indeed, I suggest that the criticism of racial preference as unfair to adversely affected whites is not without merit. The relevant point is not that such preference be abandoned but rather that it be implemented differently.

According to the desert claim, whites either have been responsible for racism or have passively benefited from it. Let us examine the responsibility claim first.

Certainly no one has demonstrated that all whites, or even a majority, are responsible for racism. How then shall the culpable whites be identified? Many employers and unions have certainly engaged in either overt racism or avoidable neutral practices that obviously excluded blacks. Perhaps they should pay the cost

---

enacting minimum-wage laws and so forth. Libertarians such as Robert Nozick, however, could consistently claim such employer entitlement only for those employers who have either acquired their enterprises through efforts that satisfy an acceptable principle of justice or who received them (e.g., by inheritance) from individuals whose original acquisition and transfer satisfy these principles. But I know of no plausible historical evidence to show that, generally speaking, American private enterprises have been acquired and transferred in accordance with such moral principles. Absent such evidence, a libertarian endorsement of any general moral entitlement by private entrepreneurs today, over employment conditions in their firms, lacks a libertarian justification.

15. Thomas Nagel, Introduction to *Equality and Preferential Treatment*, ed. Marshall Cohen, Thomas Nagel, and Thomas Scanlon (Princeton, N.J.: Princeton University Press, 1977), p. viii.

16. Steven S. Schwarzschild, "American History, Marked by Racism," *New Politics* 1 (1987): 56–58.

of discrimination remedies by, for example, continuing to pay blacks laid off by race-neutral seniority? But, on the other hand, some employers and union officials were not responsible for racist injury to blacks, and they do not deserve to pay the cost of a remedy for racism.

Similar problems arise when we attempt to identify those who passively benefited from racist practices. Let us assume that such beneficiaries do bear a measure of culpability for racism. How can we mark them out?

The salient fact is that white workers have *both* gained and lost from racism. On the one hand, the benefits to white workers from racism—overt and institutional—are undeniable. As a group, they have been first in line for hiring, training, promotion, and desirable job assignment, but last in line for seniority-based layoff. As white, they have also benefited from housing discrimination in areas where jobs could be had and from the racist impact of selection based on personal connections, seniority, and qualifications. Indeed many white candidates fail to realize that their superior qualifications may be due to their having attended predominantly white schools.

On the other hand, white workers have also lost because of racism. As a divisive force, racism harms labor, both black and white. Since blacks have more reason to fear management reprisal, they are less unwilling to work under excessive strain or for lower wages. This attitude, although quite understandable, makes it more difficult for labor, white as well as black, to attain better working conditions. I give two illustrations:

In the early 1970s a speedup was established in an auto factory whereby jobs performed by a unit of whites were assigned to a smaller group of blacks. The heavier work load then became the norm for everyone. White workers who complained were told that if they couldn't do the job, there were people who would.[17]

17. Victor Perlo, *Economics of Racism U.S.A.* (New York: International Publishers, 1975), p. 172.

In 1969, an AT&T vice president informed the assembled presidents of all Bell companies: "We must have access to an ample supply of people who will work at comparatively low rates of pay. . . . That means lots of black people." He explained that, of the persons available to work for "as little as four to five thousand a year," two-thirds were black.[18]

The willingness of blacks to accept lower wages and adverse working conditions reduces labor's bargaining power generally with management.

Racism also has inhibited the formation of trade unions. In the South, racism, because it impedes union organization, contributed to the low wage level of both white and black workers. Also some northern employers, attracted by cheaper labor costs, moved their plants—with their jobs—to the South. A labor historian summed up the divisive effect of racism: "Hiring black laborers . . . fit[s] conveniently into the anti-union efforts of many industrialists. . . . A labor force divided along ethnic and racial lines poses great difficulties for union organizers; by importing blacks, a cheap work force could be gained and unionization efforts weakened at the same time.[19]

On the whole, some white workers have lost and some have gained from racism. But to disentangle the two groups is a practical impossibility; the blameworthy cannot be marked off from the innocent.

Compensating Whites for Black Preferential Treatment

In some situations compensation by innocent parties appears to be morally acceptable. For example, Germans born after

18. "A Unique Competence": A Study of Equal Employment Opportunity in the Bell System, prepared by the Equal Employment Opportunity Commission, 1972.

19. Clement T. Imhoff, "The Recruiter," in Working Lives, ed. Marc S. Miller (New York: Pantheon, 1974), p. 56. For a comprehensive analysis of Marxian views of racial antagonisms within the working class, see Boxill, chap. 3.

World War II surely have no responsibility for the Holocaust, yet they pay taxes that fund reparations for Jewish victims. These Germans, however, pay a not exorbitant monetary assessment, but an individual white worker affected by preferential treatment loses a promotion or a job, surely a significant difference.

Someone must bear the cost of overcoming the evil of racism, but preferential treatment does seem to distribute that burden unfairly. Whites adversely affected by such treatment do appear *singled out* for sacrifice, while others—among whom are perpetrators of racism—pay nothing. The singling-out issue arises in two kinds of situations, in layoff and in hiring and advancement.

Layoff. If AA is to be effective, it must include measures that protect black employees from layoffs induced by poor business conditions. However, the sacrifice for white workers who are deprived of their jobs as a result of preferential retention of blacks is serious. Hence, wherever possible, alternatives to layoff which reduce the burden or spread it more equitably over the work force should be utilized. Among such alternatives are deferred salary arrangements (which in 1991 helped prevent teacher layoffs in New York City), payless holidays, early retirement incentives for older workers, and work-sharing. See the work-sharing example on page 44. Since the reduced work disbenefit is distributed equitably among all the employees of Smith and Co. through a reduced work week and partial unemployment insurance, neither blacks nor whites suffer disproportionate injury.

Where work-sharing or other measures that avoid or reduce layoffs is impossible, the adverse effect of seniority-based layoff on blacks can be decreased by a preferential treatment measure: At Smith and Co., 20 percent of the whites and 20 percent of the blacks would be laid off by seniority within their racial group; hence the layoff burden is shared equally by whites and blacks. Since blacks as a group are less senior than whites, however, some blacks who retain their jobs will be less senior than some whites who lose them.

The singling-out effect of such preferential treatment on white employees can be diminished by substantial monetary awards, funded by the federal government to supplement unemployment insurance. Such financial awards are important not only because many workers are far from affluent, but also because they would tend to minimize opposition to preferential retention.[20]

Compensation funded by a federal progressive tax would distribute the cost of a racially preferential remedy equitably throughout society. Taxes levied according to ability to pay best accord with the moral principle of fairness. Those whom payment hurts least, pay more. If payment for such measures (or, for that matter, for other social programs exemplifying fairness) were made by the wealthiest individuals, the unpopularity of further taxation would be greatly reduced. A federal progressive tax could also serve to spread the burden of payment for other AA measures, for example, to fund subsidies to employers for whom transporting minority workers from inner cities or the introduction of job-related testing is too costly.

Hiring and Promotion. Preferential treatment in hiring is exemplified when a basically qualified black is selected over a more qualified white; preferential treatment in promotion occurs when

---

20. For determining the specifics of awards to more senior white workers who lose their jobs because of racial preference during layoff, the *Vulcan* decision is instructive: "The court also concludes that those firefighters who have or will forfeit their seniority rights as a result of the affirmative action plan . . . ought to be compensated [by] . . . the federal government. . . . The amount of such compensation must, however, be 'just.' It is not intended to be a lifetime pension. Those senior firefighters who are laid off as a result of the affirmative action plan shall be under a duty to mitigate damages, by seeking to obtain other employment. Any claim for compensation shall be reduced by the amount of salaries or any benefits received as a result of such layoff. Moreover, the period of compensation shall end upon the attainment of other employment, but absent exceptional circumstances, no later than one year from the date of layoff" (*Vulcan Pioneers v. New Jersey Department of Civil Service,* 34 Fair Empl. Prac. Cas. [BNA] 1247–48 [D.N.J. 1984]).

a less qualified black is promoted or, where seniority determines promotion, when a black is advanced over a more senior employee. Although failure to gain a position or promotion is less serious than losing one's current job, the disbenefit of such singling out for affected whites is still significant. Monetary compensation to those whites, again funded by a progressive tax, appears to be a reasonable measure. Compensation, however, is a problem, because there is an important difference between seniority cases and qualifications cases—whether they involve promotion, hiring, or layoff. When preference is accorded to less senior blacks, the identity of the adversely affected, more senior whites is evident. Determining which white workers would be entitled to the financial awards I have proposed is an easy matter.

In qualifications cases, however, it is often not easy to determine which candidate, absent preferential treatment for blacks, would have been selected from among all the applicants. Does the past history of the firm or department show a clear commitment to the best-qualified candidate? Or were some candidates selected because they pandered to supervisors or knew how to use their influential contacts or because their ability posed no threat to mediocre incumbents?

Also, unless the qualifications criteria are themselves clear and objective, it would be very difficult to prove that one is the best qualified among all the candidates.

Hence in qualification cases monetary awards to rejected whites are reasonable only if there is already in place a clear selection criterion, such as a test, a Ph.d, or a blind review of research that makes it evident who, absent racial preference, would have been selected from all the candidates.

Care should be taken, however, to prevent abuse of the right to such monetary compensation. For example, those who claim such payment should demonstrate that they unsuccessfully sought equivalent employment and that their application for this position is reasonable given their employment skills. Hence highly educated whites would not apply for unskilled positions in order to be eligible for such compensation. Also a once-in-a-lifetime limit on all compensatory financial awards appears reasonable.

Meritocratic Critics

Some AA critics, whom I shall call meritocrats, believe that justice in the workplace is exemplified by selection according to merit standards. Hence they claim that racial preference violates the rights of more qualified white candidates. Note the difference between the meritocratic argument and the singling-out criticism I have just discussed. The meritocratic claim implies that the rights of rejected, more qualified whites are violated only because they are better qualified. Hence the meritocratic argument, unlike the singling-out criticism, has no bearing on racial preference in seniority-based selection.

Before we appraise the meritocratic criticism, a digression from the issue of preferential treatment will be useful. The meritocratic view conflicts with AA only when operative standards of competence are reduced by AA preference; however, there is a widespread perception that (seniority aside), all AA measures conflict with merit criteria. Hence I will show at the outset that certain types of AA, including some apparently preferential measures, actually raise the level of job performance. I then appraise the meritocratic criticism where it does apply, that is, to cases where preferential treatment would reduce competence on the job.

As indicated earlier, according to the employment guidelines upheld in *Griggs* (but now weakened), qualification requirements having exclusionary racial impact must pinpoint abilities needed for job performance. When enforced, these guidelines created increased interest in ensuring that such job requirements really measure ability to do the job. Thus one of the most compelling reasons for concern that licensing examinations be effective competence measures has been enforcement of these guidelines. According to a survey reported in the *New York Times,* such enforcement has contributed to a "concerted effort" by "occupational and professional groups" to ensure that their certification tests are "job relevant."[21] In 1986 the executive officer of the American Psychological Association stated: "On the specific issues addressed in the Guidelines, . . . psychologists generally agree that the caliber of employment practices in organizations has improved dramatically since [their 1978] publication."[22]

As a consequence of AA programs, black children see more black persons as teachers, administrators, and professionals. Having such role models tends to improve the self-image, vocational aspirations, and learning ability of black students, thereby increasing the pool of qualified candidates available for training and employment, a development that is likely to raise merit standards.

Some AA measures, then, such as permitting only job-related testing, improve job-selection processes. But what, generally speaking, has been the effect of AA on work performance? According to economist Jonathan S. Leonard, while productivity estimates based on direct tests are too imprecise for a compelling

21. Nancy Rubin, "Consumer and Government Forces Pushing for Job Competency Tests," *New York Times,* November 11, 1979.

22. *Oversight Hearings on EEOC's Proposed Modification of Enforcement Regulations, Including Uniform Guidelines on Employee Selection Procedures,* Hearings before the Subcommittee on Employment Opportunities of the Committee on Education and Labor, House of Representatives (Washington, D.C.: U.S. Government Printing Office 1986), p. 211. Ronald Dworkin, a legal philosopher writing on the *Bakke* case, makes a similar point about racially preferential admissions to medical school. "If [merit] . . . means . . . that a medical school should choose candidates that it supposes will make the most useful doctors, then everything turns on the judgement of what factors make different doctors useful. . . . black skin may be a socially useful trait in particular circumstances." ("Why Bakke Has No Case," *New York Review of Books,* November 10, 1977: 13–14).

conclusion either way, such tests of the effect of AA in increasing employment opportunities for blacks show no significant evidence of a productivity decline.[23]

Let us return now to a consideration of the meritocratic critique that focuses solely on preferential treatment. Whatever the effect of AA measures in their entirety, it is true that racial preference for a less qualified black can, in specific situations, reduce effective job performance. According to meritocrats, such selection violates the rights of adversely affected white candidates. Thus the philosopher Alan Goldman states:

> Unless reverse discrimination violates some *presently accepted rule for hiring* it will not be seriously unjust in the current social context. . . . The *currently accepted* rule which I believe to be just is that of *hiring by competence*. . . . In addition to its vast utility, competence is some barometer of prior effort. Thus society, it seems, does have a right in the name of welfare and equal opportunity to impose a rule for hiring, and the general rule ought to be hiring the most competent. This means that those individuals who attain maximal competence for various positions acquire rights through their efforts to those positions. (emphases added)[24]

Let us assume that insofar as maximally qualified candidates have exerted effort to attain positions under an accepted and just rule, they have a prima facie right to such positions. But the fact is that, contrary to Goldman, hiring the most competent candidate is not the "currently accepted" rule in employment. Being the most qualified candidate is indeed one way to get the job, but employers' ignoring of merit standards and their explicit preference for specific groups are widespread. Merit criteria are either ignored or undermined in several ways.

23. Jonathan S. Leonard, "The Impact of Affirmative Action Regulation and Equal Employment Law on Black Employment," *Journal of Economic Perspectives* 4 (1990): 61–62.

24. Alan Goldman, "Limits to the Justification of Reverse Discrimination," *Social Theory and Practice* 3 (1975): 289–91.

In accordance with a traditional legal principle—employment "at will"—private U.S. employers have had the right to discharge their workers without a reasonable cause based on work performance. This principle gives employers the legal right to dismiss qualified employees merely for refusing to support political candidates of the employer's choice or for expressing unpopular views on the job or even in the privacy of their own homes. An employer right to arbitrary discharge without reasonable cause is hardly compatible with a merit system. Although the employer's right to discharge is now restricted by specific exceptions identified in union contracts and in federal and state laws (e.g., prohibiting race and sex discrimination), employment at will is still a significant legal principle in U.S. courts.[25]

Competent job performance has also been undermined by the widespread use of unvalidated employment tests and irrelevant subjective standards for hiring and promotion.

As I described earlier, federal and state governments have continuously given employment preference to veterans, thereby excluding large numbers of more qualified nonveterans.

Many employees obtain their vocational qualifications in colleges and professional schools. In some such institutions preference for admission has been extended to children of alumni. After Allan Bakke sued the University of California medical school, it was revealed that the dean had been permitted to select some admittees without reference to the usual screening process. As one writer noted, "The dean's 'special admissions program' was evidently devoted to the *realpolitik* of sustaining influential support for the school."[26]

Seniority-based selection for training, promotion, and retention in layoff is commonly practiced in both the private and

25. *Coppage v. Kansas,* 236 U.S. 441 (1914); Burton Hall, "Collective Bargaining and Workers' Liberty," in *Moral Rights in the Workplace,* ed. Gertrude Ezorsky (New York: State University of New York Press, 1987), pp. 161–65.

26. Allan P. Sindler, *Bakke, DeFunis, and Minority Admissions* (New York: Longman, 1978), p. 69n. This practice was ended in 1977.

public sector of the economy. Such selection is based on years of service, not evaluation of job performance. Adherence to meritocratic principles would in some situations require the abolition of seniority criteria for reward.

As emphasized earlier, reliance on personal connections is probably the most widely used recruitment method in American employment, a practice that often works against a merit system. An incumbent's graduate-school friend, the boss's nephew, or a political-patronage appointee is frequently not the most qualified person available for the job.

Note too that gaining promotion through social networks within the firm may have a corrupting effect on job performance as well as on moral character. The employee may see pandering to the right people as the best route to success.

Because traditionally accepted preference is so widespread, some blacks selected by AA preference may in fact replace less-qualified whites who would have been chosen by such traditional preference.

I conclude that merit selection is not, as Goldman claims, the currently accepted rule. Goldman states, however, that unless preferential treatment violates a currently accepted rule it is not "seriously unjust."[27] In that case, preferential treatment is not seriously unjust.

A different version of the meritocratic claim might be that although hiring the best candidate is not the currently accepted rule and because (as Goldman says) merit selection has social utility, such selection *ought* to be the rule, and thus preferential treatment should not be extended to blacks. According to this meritocratic claim, all practices that often conflict with merit standards, such as selection by seniority ranking, veteran status, and powerful personal connections, should be eliminated. In that case, why not begin the struggle for merit in American employ-

27. See Goldman.

ment by calling for an end to these practices? Why start by excluding members of a largely poor and powerless group, such as black people?

Let us focus on the consequences simply of denying preference to basically qualified blacks. Let us assume that this denial would produce some gain in social utility, that is, efficiency. That benefit would, I suggest, weigh very little in the moral balance against the double accomplishment of preferential treatment: compensation to blacks for past wrongs against them and achieving what this nation has never known—occupational integration, racial justice in the workplace.

Preferential Treatment and Black Self-Respect

Some commentators suggest that preferential treatment may be morally injurious to black persons. Thus Midge Decter and the economist Thomas Sowell worry that preference damages the self-respect of blacks.[28]

Does preference really injure the self-respect of those it benefits? Traditional preference extended to personal connections has occasioned no such visible injury to self-respect. Career counselors who advise job seekers to develop influential contacts exhibit no fear that their clients will think less well of themselves; indeed, job candidates who secure powerful connections count themselves *fortunate*.

It might be objected that blacks (or any persons) who gain their positions through preferential treatment ought to respect themselves less. But this claim assumes that these blacks do not deserve such treatment. I believe that, because the overwhelming majority of blacks has been grievously wronged by racism, they deserve to be compensated for such injury and that black benefi-

28. Midge Decter, *New York Times*, op-ed, July 6, 1980; Thomas Sowell, "'Affirmative Action' Reconsidered," *Public Interest* no. 42 (1976): 64.

ciaries of employment preference—like veterans compensated by employment preference—have no good reason to feel unworthy.

Moreover, telling blacks—the descendants of slaves—that they ought to feel unworthy of their preferential positions can become self-fulfilling prophecy. Where are the black persons whose spirit and self-confidence have not already suffered because of the palpable barriers to attending white schools, living in white neighborhoods, and enjoying relations of friendship and intimacy with white people? Those blacks who, despite all the obstacles of overt and institutional racism, have become basically qualified for their positions should be respected for that achievement. Justice Marshall reminds us that the history of blacks differs from that of other ethnic groups. It includes not only slavery but also its aftermath, in which as a people they were marked inferior by our laws, a mark that has endured.[29] Opportunities created by preferential treatment should symbolize an acknowledgment of such injustice and a commitment to create a future free of racism.

29. *Regents of University of California* v. *Bakke,* 438 U.S. 265 (1978) (Marshall, J., concurring in part and dissenting in part).

Part 3

Documents

5

Overt and Institutional Racism

*"A Unique Competence": A Study of Equal
Employment Opportunity in the Bell System,* prepared
by the Equal Employment Opportunity Commission,
92d Cong., 2d Sess., 118 Cong. Rec. 4507 (1972)
[Excerpt]

What had been in the past at the Bell system was the relative
exclusion of black workers from employment in the Bell operating companies except in the lowest paying and most undesirable
blue collar jobs.

Even today there are blacks who toil in service worker or
laborer jobs who were not able to obtain any better positions
when hired by Bell decades ago. More importantly, the present
gross underrepresentation of black workers in desirable craft and
management jobs is directly attributable to their past exclusion
from most entry-level positions. Finally, many of the institutional
practices which contributed to the exclusion in the past are still
being used.

.

[T]he occupational distribution of black employees in the Bell System followed a uniform pattern, regardless of the total employment figures for blacks in any particular company. Whether in the West, North, East or South, in the 1960's black employees at Bell companies were primarily females classified as "office and clerical" employees. The pattern of black occupational distribution which first emerged in the 1940's in the East was, by 1969, evident in all areas. *Somehow,* black employment was being concentrated in the lowest-paying, least-desirable, dead-end jobs in the Bell System. Blacks still had not obtained a significant number of high-paying craft jobs in any area. This fact emphasizes the futility of the employment advances made by blacks in the Bell System since 1930.

Economic factors affecting black employment

As noted before, the chief chronicler of black employment at the Bell System, Dr. Bernard Anderson, has concluded that labor market conditions in the North and East were a major, if not primary, force contributing to the increased employment of blacks as Operators during the 1950's. Other evidence, not available to Dr. Anderson, demonstrates conclusively that the same economic forces at work during the 1950's continued in the 1960's to push up the employment of blacks in the Operator job, especially in large SMSA's with sizable black populations.[1] In the last 10 years turn-over among Operators has continued to escalate, reaching astounding levels in major urban areas. It is these areas that are becoming increasingly black and in which the Operator's wage is no longer attractive to whites. The combination of these factors is rapidly converting the Traffic Department from simply a "nunnery" into a "ghetto nunnery."

This conclusion has been reached repeatedly by persons at the

1. The commonly used unit for measuring economic, employment, labor market, and population trends of urban areas is the Standard Metropolitan Statistical Area (SMSA).

highest levels within the Bell System itself. In October 1969, an extremely important "Report on Force Loss and the Urban Labor Market" was presented by AT&T Vice President Walter Straley to the assembled Presidents of all Bell companies. According to the report, "What a telephone company needs to know about its labor market (is) who is available for work paying as little as $4000 to $5000 a year." According to Straley's remarks, two out of three persons available at that wage were black: "It is therefore just a plain fact that in today's world, telephone company wages are more in line with black expectations—and the tighter the labor market the more this is true." The report continues:

"Population and labor force projections are not at all encouraging. The kind of people we need are going to be in very short supply. . . . Most of our new hires go into entry level jobs which means we must have access to an ample supply of people who will work at comparatively low rates of pay. That means city people more so than suburbanites. That means lots of black people.

"There are not enough white, middle class, success-oriented men and women in the labor force—or at least that portion of the labor force available to the telephone companies—to supply our requirements for craft and occupational people. And from now on, the number of such people who are available will grow smaller even as our need becomes greater. It is therefore perfectly plain that we need nonwhite employees, not because we are good citizens. Or because it is the law as well as a national goal to give them employment. We need them because we have so many jobs to fill and they will take them."

•   •   •   •

To recapitulate, the increased black employment during the 1960's was dictated by labor market conditions which forced the Bell System to hire black females as Operators. Similar economic factors did not apply to Plant craft jobs and consequently few black males were hired. It is reasonable, therefore, to conclude that the Bell System hired blacks only when there were no economically viable alternatives.

. . . .

Black employment in the Bell System increased steadily from the virtual exclusion of the 1930's and 1940's to an all-time high at the end of the 1960's. Yet, even at that time, most Bell companies had still not reached the average level of black employment for all major companies in their respective operating areas.

Most of the increase in black employment from the 1940's to the end of the 1960's came in a low-paying, dead-end, and otherwise highly undesirable job, that of Operator. Very few blacks obtained jobs as craft workers.

Even this increase has not been uniform throughout the System; the Southern companies—Southern Bell, South Central Bell, Southwestern Bell, and C&P (Va.)—continued their exclusionist policies up to the mid-1960's and consequently lagged far behind the rest of the system.

Even the companies with the best and most sustained efforts of black employment (New York Tel., Ohio Bell, Bell of Pa., Michigan Bell, Illinois Bell, and Pacific Tel.) did not, after decades of hiring blacks, have a significant number of black workers in management.

. . . .

The Bell System's poor record of black employment is particularly disturbing in view of the fact that each year large numbers of persons are hired in major urban areas for jobs requiring little, if any, skills.

. . . . There is no correlation between the penetration rate of blacks in the Bell System and their occupational position;

whether a company employs many or few black workers, those workers are concentrated in the lowest paying jobs. This phenomenon is largely attributable to the fact that the blacks in *all* Bell companies are disproportionately employed as Operators.

These findings are frightening. No Bell company has yet provided blacks with true equality. New York Tel. and Pacific Tel. may hire thousands of blacks, but they are no better off than the few blacks in Mobile. They are all locked into low paying jobs.

Overrepresentation of black females

. . . At the end of 1970, every Bell company had a substantial overrepresentation of females in its black work force in contrast to its white force. . . . This should not, by any stretch of the imagination, be taken to mean that black females are well employed. As noted before, they have the lowest-paying major job in the System. Since "female" jobs are appropriately identical to low-paying jobs, it is no surprise that when blacks entered the System in substantial numbers, they would be black females. "Male" jobs are higher-paying and more rewarding. Just as white females have been kept out of this preserve, so also have all blacks, male *and* female.

The fact that most blacks in the Bell System are female has two important implications. First, *all* companies have a long way to go in terms of affording equal opportunity to black males. Second, most blacks in the Bell system suffer a double handicap of *race* and sex.

The myriad Bell System policies which discriminate against females because of their sex also clearly affect blacks much more than whites. . . . .

The evidence for December 31, 1970 demonstrates the inexorable effect of the [historical] occupational trends. . . . The early relegation of blacks to laborer and service worker jobs is reflected in the fact that a black is still 5 1/2 times more likely to wind up a janitor than is a white. A black is also 3 times more likely to be an Operator. But the high-paying craft jobs are an entirely different story. A black has less than half a chance that a white has of obtaining one of those jobs. Thus, it is absolutely clear that blacks are not randomly distributed in all jobs. The concentration of blacks in the least desirable jobs and the relative exclusion of blacks from the best jobs certainly does not support Bell's claim of leadership. On the contrary, the evidence would support exactly the opposite conclusion.

Summary

Thirty years after the Bell System first began to desegregate and six and one-half years after equal employment became the law of the land, Bell companies in most of the 30 SMSA's still employed blacks at a rate less than that of the population or lower even than the average of all major employers.

—The companies in the South had failed by large measure to match even the minimal efforts of the rest of the System.

—Those black workers that have been employed in the Bell System have been largely relegated to the lowest paying, least desirable jobs in the companies.

—The black worker does not have an equal chance to be hired, and, if hired, he or she does not have an equal chance to get the best jobs.

—Most blacks in the Bell System are female and thus suffer from a dual handicap of both race and sex.

BELL SYSTEM PRACTICES AS THEY AFFECT BLACKS

[T]he low overall participation rate of blacks in most Bell System companies, relative both to the area all-industry average or the population, is quite surprising for three reasons. First, due to extraordinarily high turnover among non-management employees, the Bell System hires approximately two hundred thousand persons every year. Second, Bell System employment is concentrated in SMSA's which contain the bulk of the black population in the United States. Third, virtually all of the new employees hired by Bell System companies each year possess minimal job skills.

The conflux of these elements would lead one to expect that in almost every SMSA the black participation rate would have long ago surpassed the all-industry average. But, of course, this did not happen. The low utilization of blacks in the South is easily explained by deliberate racially discriminatory hiring practices. Elsewhere, the lag in reaching the all-industry average is largely explained by Bell System pre-employment criteria which tend to *screen out blacks* and *screen in whites*. Two criteria—paper credentials and test scores—are of paramount importance.

. . . .

No employer can lawfully utilize hiring criteria which systematically reject a disparate number of blacks without any evidence that the criteria are valid predictors of job success. And yet, the nation's largest private employer does just that.

In summary, part of the explanation for the below average black participation rate in most Bell companies lies in the educational requirements imposed by company policy. These educational requirements have had and continue to have a disparate impact on blacks and suppress black employment to a level considerably lower than it otherwise would be. The preference which Bell System paper credential requirements give to whites has been reduced over time, but significant impediments to black employment in craft, Service Representative and sales jobs still exist. No evidence has ever been presented that these paper credential requirements reliably relate to job performance.

.

[T]he Bell System testing practices constitute a major barrier to increased black employment in the Bell System. Under these circumstances, continued use of such tests can be justified only if they validly predict who will and who will not perform satisfactorily on the job. Although the Bell System has conducted at least 27 studies of its test batteries, these studies contain virtually no evidence that the tests accurately predict job performance. In the absence of substantial empirical evidence of job-related validity, the Bell System's test batteries cannot lawfully be used to screen out blacks.

. . . Considering the very great advantage obtained by whites solely on the basis of the Bell System's paper and pencil tests, it is small wonder that the Bell System has lagged substantially behind other industries in employing blacks. Although Bell System companies have hired approximately two million unskilled workers in the last decade, most of them in SMSA's with massive black populations, paper credential prerequisites and test score requirements have acted to keep blacks from obtaining a proportionate share of telephone company jobs. The fact that by 1971 many SMSA's had finally equaled the all-industry average for over-all black participation by employing blacks as Operators is almost exclusively a function of the labor market conditions discussed below.

.

The low pay is not, however, the only undesirable feature of the Operator job. Working conditions, apparently, are virtually intolerable. The job itself is "highly routine," and nothing but a "structured and repetitive task." A study prepared for Southwestern Bell by Dr. George Robinson of the Graduate School of Business, Washington University, concluded as follows:

"There is a fairly general feeling among the operators, both those remaining and those resigning, that their job is dull and uninteresting. The most typical comment was that the job is highly regimented, affording little opportunity for self-expression or self-fulfillment."

In addition, the Bell System rigidly enforces "formal rules covering every aspect" of the Operator's job. There are stringent rules governing dress, conversation at the switchboard, phraseology, and clerical accuracy; but the most abrasive and particularly inflexible rules are those governing absenteeism and tardiness. A report prepared in August, 1970, by the Southwest Research Institute in Houston declared that, "Concern over attendance has grown beyond all proportion within the system. Attendance is so important that the Company has lost its perspective."

The "authoritarian manner" in which the attendance and tardiness rules are enforced is exacerbated by the fact that low seniority Operators are required to work divided shifts, "unenviable schedules involving an early morning shift and a late evening shift, separated by a period long enough to require a return home in the middle of the working day." Moreover, most Operators are required to work staggered schedules, including many weekends.

The impact of all of these undesirable features of the Operator's job is cumulative. The 1970 Southwest Research Institute report described the overall results as follows:

"(Operators are quick to describe) the noxious demands of work that is too highly structured, their loss of personal identity, their lack of freedom to rely on their own judgement, their difficulty in becoming part of a cohesive social group, and the absence of any reasonable hope for future advancement.... They are necessary parts of a system designed by geniuses for execution by idiots."

Turnover. Under such circumstances, it is hardly surprising that turnover among Operators is very high.

. . . .

Viewed from any angle, all available evidence leads to the conclusion that the concentration of blacks into the Operator job is no accident. It is the direct result of deliberate company policies adopted in response to the compelling problems created by the high turnover among Operators and the low wages offered to attract applicants to the job. There is no doubt that AT&T is attempting to solve this problem by maintaining the low wages and hiring blacks who will work for a wage which whites shun.

Bell system practices which frustrate the movement of blacks out of the Operator's job

Most blacks in the Bell System suffer from a double handicap—they are at once both *black* and *female* and the Bell companies have never been overly generous in their treatment of either group. As the Bell companies move into the 1970s, black females continue to pour *into* and *out of* the job of Operator.

Because Operator has, since the days of Emma Nutt, been a female job, it has been cut off from the mainstream of movement upward within the System. The consistent high turn-over among Operators has reinforced AT&T's natural inclination not to transfer or promote Operators to better jobs. AT&T obviously decided that vacancies due to "dismissals" and resignations were numerous enough without creating additional vacancies by promotion and transfer.

The evidence surely indicates that System policy continues to follow this circular pattern. The Operator job is, quite pointedly, a *horrendous* job. No greater testimony to this fact exists than the unbelievably high rate at which employees bolt from the job. The Bell System's response is amazing: rather than restructure the job, improve the wages, and provide important new avenues for promotion and transfer—changes which even common sense would suggest—AT&T has decided to keep the wages depressed and simply hire more and more black females.

The inevitable effects of these policy decisions are all too ominous. Most of the blacks in the Bell System will never have a real chance at a good job. The economic realities of the labor market will force large numbers of blacks to apply for Operator jobs. After all, *any* job is better than no job; any job except Operator. The realities of the Operator job will thus force blacks to quit as fast as they are forced to apply. They will never stay long enough to get a promotion or a transfer, *even if* such opportunities existed. This sad situation appears to be AT&T's major answer to the cries for equal opportunity.

CONCLUDING COMMENTS ON BLACKS IN THE BELL SYSTEM

An overview of the history of black employment in the Bell System leads to one very hard fact: in no Bell company are blacks on an equal footing with whites. Throughout the South, the lingering effects of deliberate racial discrimination are readily apparent in both the small number and types of jobs blacks hold. Elsewhere, progress in black employment has meant the hiring of large numbers of black females as Operators. There are relatively few black craft workers or black managers anywhere in the System.

This pattern of black employment is the result of many factors, including a heritage of overt exclusion, labor market conditions, and irrelevant and artificially high educational and testing requirements. For whatever reason, however, the failure of the Bell System to provide real equality of opportunity for blacks must be considered a national tragedy.

In dollar terms alone, the discrimination against blacks takes a heavy toll. Because blacks are not employed in numbers proportional to their percentage in the population and because those that are employed work in low-paying jobs, each year blacks in 30 SMSA's lose over $225 million.

. . . It would be a mistake, however, to calculate the effects of discrimination in terms of lost wages alone. Judge Gewin, of the United States Court of Appeals for the Fifth Circuit, has eloquently described the intangible results of racially discriminatory employment practices.

Those who love their work may sometimes forget that a successful human community requires the performance of many vapid and colorless tasks. Even the most tedious physical labor is endurable and in a sense enjoyable, however, when the laborer knows that his work will be appreciated and his work rewarded. "Work without hope," said Coleridge, "draws nectar in a sieve, and hope without an object cannot live." The ethic which permeates the American dream is that a person may advance as far as his talents and his merit will carry him. And it is unthinkable that a citizen of this great country should be relegated to unremitting toil with never a glimmer of light in the midnight of it all.

6

Remedies for Institutional Racism

Set-Asides for Minority Contractors Denied

City of Richmond v. J. A. Croson Co., 488 U.S. 469
(1989) (Marshall, J., dissenting) [Excerpt]

The City of Richmond adopted a Minority Business Utilization Plan
requiring that at least 30 percent of the dollar amount of the city's
construction contracts would go to minority business enterprises. A
waiver to this 30 percent set-aside would be granted only if there were
proof that qualified minority enterprises were either unavailable or
unwilling to participate. J. A. Croson Co. brought a suit against the
city after it was denied a waiver on a project in which it was the only
bidder. The Supreme Court affirmed that the city had failed to demonstrate a compelling governmental interest justifying the plan, since the
facts supporting the plan did not establish the type of identified past
discrimination in the city's construction industry which would au-
thorize race-based relief under the Fourteenth Amendment's Equal
Protection Clause. Justice Marshall, however, joined by Justice Brennan and Justice Blackmun, dissented:

. . . Richmond has two powerful interests in setting aside a
portion of public contracting funds for minority-owned enter-

prises. The first is the city's interest in eradicating the effects of past racial discrimination.

·

Richmond has a second compelling interest in setting aside, where possible, a portion of its contracting dollars. That interest is the prospective one of preventing the city's own spending decisions from reinforcing and perpetuating the exclusionary effects of past discrimination.

·

When government channels all its contracting funds to a white dominated community of established contractors whose racial homogeneity is the product of private discrimination, it does more than place its *imprimatur* on the practices which forged and which continue to define that community. It also provides a measurable boost to those economic entities that have thrived within it, while denying important economic benefits to those entities which, but for prior discrimination, might well be better qualified to receive valuable government contracts. In my view, the interest in ensuring that the government does not reflect and reinforce prior private discrimination in dispensing public contracts is every bit as strong as the interest in eliminating private discrimination—an interest which this Court has repeatedly deemed compelling.

·

Richmond acted against a backdrop of congressional and Executive Branch studies which demonstrated with such force the nationwide pervasiveness of prior discrimination that Congress presumed that "present economic inequities" in construction contracting resulted from "past discriminatory systems." Supra, at 4 (quoting H.R. Rep. No. 94-468, pp. 1–2 (1975)). The city's local evidence confirmed that Richmond's construction industry did not deviate from this pernicious national pattern. The fact that just 0.67% of public construction expenditures over the previous five years had gone to minority-owned prime contractors, despite the city's racially mixed population, strongly suggests that construction contracting in the area was rife with "present economic inequities." To the extent this enormous disparity did not itself demonstrate that discrimination had occurred, the descriptive testimony of Richmond's elected and appointed leaders drew the necessary link between the pitifully small presence of minorities in construction contracting and past exclusionary practices. That *no one* who testified challenged this depiction of widespread racial discrimination in area construction contracting lent significant weight to these accounts. The fact that area trade associations had virtually no minority members dramatized the extent of present inequities and suggested the lasting power of past discriminatory systems.

Validation of Qualification Requirements

Griggs v. Duke Power Co., 401 U.S. 424 (1971)

Black employees at Duke Power Co. brought an action claiming that the plant's requirement for a high school diploma or intelligence test as a condition of employment or transfer violated the Civil Rights Act of 1964. The District Court's decision to deny this action was reversed in part by the Court of Appeals. However, the Supreme Court held that the act requires that (1) arbitrary barriers to employment operating to discriminate on the basis of race should be eliminated; and (2) testing procedures should not have controlling force unless they can be shown to be a reasonable measure of job performance.

Documents

We granted the writ in this case to resolve the question whether an employer is prohibited by the Civil Rights Act of 1964, Title VII, from requiring a high school education or passing of a standardized general intelligence test as a condition of employment in or transfer to jobs when (a) neither standard is shown to be significantly related to successful job performance, (b) both requirements operate to disqualify Negroes at a substantially higher rate than white applicants, and (c) the jobs in question formerly had been filled only by white employees as part of a longstanding practice of giving preference to whites.[1]

Congress provided, in Title VII of the Civil Rights Act of 1964, for class actions for enforcement of provisions of the Act and this proceeding was brought by a group of incumbent Negro employees against Duke Power Company. All the petitioners are employed at the Company's Dan River Steam Station, a power generating facility located at Draper, North Carolina. At the time this action was instituted, the Company had 95 employees at the Dan River Station, 14 of whom were Negroes; 13 of these are petitioners here.

The District Court found that prior to July 2, 1965, the effective date of the Civil Rights Act of 1964, the Company openly discriminated on the basis of race in the hiring and assigning of employees at its Dan River plant. The plant was organized into five operating departments: (1) Labor, (2) Coal Handling, (3)

1. The Act provides:
"Sec. 703. (a) It shall be an unlawful employment practice for an employer. . .
"(2) to limit, segregate, or classify his employees in any way which would deprive or tend to deprive any individual of employment opportunities or otherwise adversely affect his status as an employee, because of such individual's race, color, religion, sex, or national origin. . . .
"(h) Notwithstanding any other provision of this title, it shall not be an unlawful employment practice for an employer . . . to give and to act upon the results of any professionally developed ability test provided that such test, its administration or action upon the results is not designed, intended or used to discrimate because of race, color, religion, sex or national origin. . . ." 78 Stat. 255, 42 U.S.C. § 2000e–2.

Operations, (4) Maintenance, and (5) Laboratory and Test. Negroes were employed only in the Labor Department where the highest paying jobs paid less than the lowest paying jobs in the other four "operating" departments in which only whites were employed.[2] Promotions were normally made within each department on the basis of job seniority. Transferees into a department usually began in the lowest position.

In 1955 the Company instituted a policy of requiring a high school education for initial assignment to any department except Labor, and for transfer from the Coal Handling to any "inside" department (Operations, Maintenance, or Laboratory). When the Company abandoned its policy of restricting Negroes to the Labor Department in 1965, completion of high school also was made a prerequisite to transfer from Labor to any other department. From the time the high school requirement was instituted to the time of trial, however, white employees hired before the time of the high school education requirement continued to perform satisfactorily and achieve promotions in the "operating" departments. Findings on this score are not challenged.

The Company added a further requirement for new employees on July 2, 1965, the date on which Title VII became effective. To qualify for placement in any but the Labor Department it became necessary to register satisfactory scores on two professionally prepared aptitude tests, as well as to have a high school education. Completion of high school alone continued to render employees eligible for transfer to the four desirable departments from which Negroes had been excluded if the incumbent had been employed prior to the time of the new requirement. In September 1965 the Company began to permit incumbent em-

---

2. A Negro was first assigned to a job in an operating department in August 1966, five months after charges had been filed with the Equal Employment Opportunity Commission. The employee, a high school graduate who had begun in the Labor Department in 1953, was promoted to a job in the Coal Handling Department.

ployees who lacked a high school education to qualify for transfer from Labor or Coal Handling to an "inside" job by passing two tests—the Wonderlic Personnel Test, which purports to measure general intelligence, and the Bennett Mechanical Comprehension Test. Neither was directed or intended to measure the ability to learn to perform a particular job or category of jobs. The requisite scores used for both initial hiring and transfer approximated the national median for high school graduates.[3]

The District Court had found that while the Company previously followed a policy of overt racial discrimination in a period prior to the Act, such conduct had ceased. The District Court also concluded that Title VII was intended to be prospective only and, consequently, the impact of prior inequities was beyond the reach of corrective action authorized by the Act.

The Court of Appeals was confronted with a question of first impression, as are we, concerning the meaning of Title VII. After careful analysis a majority of that court concluded that a subjective test of the employer's intent should govern, particularly in a close case, and that in this case there was no showing of a discriminatory purpose in the adoption of the diploma and test requirements. On this basis, the Court of Appeals concluded there was no violation of the Act.

The Court of Appeals reversed the District Court in part, rejecting the holding that residual discrimination arising from prior employment practices was insulated from remedial action.[4]

3. The test standards are thus more stringent than the high school requirement, since they would screen out approximately half of all high school graduates.

4. The Court of Appeals ruled that Negroes employed in the Labor Department at a time when there was no high school or test requirement for entrance into the higher paying departments could not now be made subject to those requirements, since whites hired contemporaneously into those departments were never subject to them. The Court of Appeals also required that the seniority rights of those Negroes be measured on a plantwide, rather than a departmental, basis. However, the Court of Appeals denied relief to the Negro employees without a high school education or its equivalent who were hired into the Labor Department after institution of the educational requirement.

The Court of Appeals noted, however, that the District Court was correct in its conclusion that there was no showing of a racial purpose or invidious intent in the adoption of the high school diploma requirement or general intelligence test and that these standards had been applied fairly to whites and Negroes alike. It held that, in the absence of a discriminatory purpose, use of such requirements was permitted by the Act. In so doing, the Court of Appeals rejected the claim that because these two requirements operated to render ineligible a markedly disproportionate number of Negroes, they were unlawful under Title VII unless shown to be job related.[5] We granted the writ on these claims. 399 U.S. 926.

The objective of Congress in the enactment of Title VII is plain from the language of the statute. It was to achieve equality of employment opportunities and remove barriers that have operated in the past to favor an identifiable group of white employees over other employees. Under the Act, practices, procedures, or tests neutral on their face, and even neutral in terms of intent, cannot be maintained if they operate to "freeze" the status quo of prior discriminatory employment practices.

The Court of Appeals' opinion, and the partial dissent, agreed that, on the record in the present case, "whites register far better on the Company's alternative requirements" than Negroes.[6] 420

5. One member of that court disagreed with this aspect of the decision, maintaining, as do the petitioners in this Court, that Title VII prohibits the use of employment criteria that operate in a racially exclusionary fashion and do not measure skills or abilities necessary to performance of the jobs for which those criteria are used.

6. In North Carolina, 1960 census statistics show that, while 34% of white males had completed high school, only 12% of Negro males had done so. U.S. Bureau of the Census, U.S. Census of Population: 1960, Vol. 1, Characteristics of the Population, pt. 35, Table 47.

Similarly, with respect to standardized tests, the EEOC in one case found that use of a battery of tests, including the Wonderlic and Bennett tests used by the Company in the instant case, resulted in 58% of whites passing the tests, as compared with only 6% of the blacks. Decision of EEOC, CCH Empl. Prac. Guide, ¶ 17,304.53 (Dec. 2, 1966). See also Decision of EEOC 70-552, CCH Empl. Prac. Guide, ¶ 6139 (Feb. 19, 1970).

F. 2d 1225, 1239 n. 6. This consequence would appear to be directly traceable to race. Basic intelligence must have the means of articulation to manifest itself fairly in a testing process. Because they are Negroes, petitioners have long received inferior education in segregated schools and this Court expressly recognized these differences in *Gaston County* v. *United States,* 395 U.S. 285 (1969). There, because of the inferior education received by Negroes in North Carolina, this Court barred the institution of a literacy test for voter registration on the ground that the test would abridge the right to vote indirectly on account of race. Congress did not intend by Title VII, however, to guarantee a job to every person regardless of qualifications. In short, the Act does not command that any person be hired simply because he was formerly the subject of discrimination, or because he is a member of a minority group. Discriminatory preference for any group, minority or majority, is precisely and only what Congress has proscribed. What is required by Congress is the removal of artificial, arbitrary, and unnecessary barriers to employment when the barriers operate invidiously to discriminate on the basis of racial or other impermissible classification.

Congress has now provided that tests or criteria for employment or promotion may not provide equality of opportunity merely in the sense of the fabled offer of milk to the stork and the fox. On the contrary, Congress has now required that the posture and condition of the job-seeker be taken into account. It has—to resort again to the fable—provided that the vessel in which the milk is proffered be one all seekers can use. The Act proscribes not only overt discrimination but also practices that are fair in form, but discriminatory in operation. The touchstone is business necessity. If an employment practice which operates to exclude Negroes cannot be shown to be related to job performance, the practice is prohibited.

On the record before us, neither the high school completion requirement nor the general intelligence test is shown to bear a demonstrable relationship to successful performance of the jobs for which it was used. Both were adopted, as the Court of Appeals noted, without meaningful study of their relationship to job-performance ability. Rather, a vice president of the Company testified, the requirements were instituted on the Company's judgment that they generally would improve the over-all quality of the work force.

The evidence, however, shows that employees who have not completed high school or taken the tests have continued to perform satisfactorily and make progress in departments for which the high school and test criteria are now used.[7] The promotion record of present employees who would not be able to meet the new criteria thus suggests the possibility that the requirements may not be needed even for the limited purpose of preserving the avowed policy of advancement within the Company. In the context of this case, it is unnecessary to reach the question whether testing requirements that take into account capability for the next succeeding position or related future promotion might be utilized upon a showing that such long-range requirements fulfill a genuine business need. In the present case the Company has made no such showing.

The Court of Appeals held that the Company had adopted the diploma and test requirements without any "intention to discriminate against Negro employees." 420 F. 2d. at 1232. We do not suggest that either the District Court or the Court of Appeals erred in examining the employer's intent; but good intent or absence of discriminatory intent does not redeem employment procedures or testing mechanisms that operate as "built-in headwinds" for minority groups and are unrelated to measuring job capability.

7. For example, between July 2, 1965, and November 14, 1966, the percentage of white employees who were promoted but who were not high school graduates was nearly identical to the percentage of nongraduates in the entire white work force.

The Company's lack of discriminatory intent is suggested by special efforts to help the undereducated employees through Company financing of two-thirds the cost of tuition for high school training. But Congress directed the thrust of the Act to the *consequences* of employment practices, not simply the motivation. More than that, Congress has placed on the employer the burden of showing that any given requirement must have a manifest relationship to the employment in question.

The facts of this case demonstrate the inadequacy of broad and general testing devices as well as the infirmity of using diplomas or degrees as fixed measures of capability. History is filled with examples of men and women who rendered highly effective performance without the conventional badges of accomplishment in terms of certificates, diplomas, or degrees. Diplomas and tests are useful servants, but Congress has mandated the commonsense proposition that they are not to become masters of reality.

The Company contends that its general intelligence tests are specifically permitted by § 703 (h) of the Act.[8] That section authorizes the use of "any professionally developed ability test" that is not "designed, intended *or used* to discriminate because of race. . . ." (Emphasis added.)

The Equal Employment Opportunity Commission, having enforcement responsibility, has issued guidelines interpreting § 703 (h) to permit only the use of job-related tests.[9] The administrative

8. Section 703 (h) applies only to tests. It has no applicability to the high school diploma requirement.

9. EEOC Guidelines on Employment Testing Procedures, issued August 24, 1966, provide:

"The Commission accordingly interprets 'professionally developed ability test' to mean a test which fairly measures the knowledge or skills required by the particular job or class of jobs which the applicant seeks, or which fairly affords the employer a chance to measure the applicant's ability to perform a particular job or class of jobs. The fact that a test was prepared by an individual or organization claiming expertise in test preparation does not, without more, justify its use within the meaning of Title VII."

The EEOC position has been elaborated in the new Guidelines on Employee

interpretation of the Act by the enforcing agency is entitled to great deference. See, e.g., *United States v. City of Chicago*, 400 U.S. 8 (1970); *Udall v. Tallman*, 380 U.S. 1 (1965); *Power Reactor Co. v. Electricians*, 367 U.S. 396 (1961). Since the Act and its legislative history support the Commission's construction, this affords good reason to treat the guidelines as expressing the will of Congress.

Section 703 (h) was not contained in the House version of the Civil Rights Act but was added in the Senate during extended debate. For a period, debate revolved around claims that the bill as proposed would prohibit all testing and force employers to hire unqualified persons simply because they were part of a group formerly subject to job discrimination.[10] Proponents of Title VII sought throughout the debate to assure the critics that the Act would have no effect on job-related tests. Senators Case of New Jersey and Clark of Pennsylvania, comanagers of the bill on the Senate floor, issued a memorandum explaining that the proposed Title VII "expressly protects the employer's right to insist that any prospective applicant, Negro or white, *must meet the applicable job qualifications.* Indeed, the very purpose of title VII is to promote hiring on the basis of job qualifications, rather than on

---

Selection Procedures, 29 CFR § 1607, 35 Fed. Reg. 12333 (Aug. 1, 1970).These guidelines demand that employers using tests have available "data demonstrating that the test is predictive of or significantly correlated with important elements of work behavior which comprise or are relevant to the job or jobs for which candidates are being evaluated." *Id.,* at § 1607.4(c).

10. The congressional discussion was prompted by the decision of a hearing examiner for the Illinois Fair Employment Commission in *Myart v. Motorola Co.* (The decision is reprinted at 110 Cong. Rec. 5662.) That case suggested that standardized tests on which whites performed better than Negroes could never be used. The decision was taken to mean that such tests could never be justified even if the needs of the business required them. A number of Senators feared that Title VII might produce a similar result. See remarks of Senators Ervin, 110 Cong. Rec. 5614–5616; Smathers, *id.,* at 5999–6000; Holland, *id.,* at 7012–7013; Hill, *id.,* at 8447; Tower, *id.,* at 9024; Talmadge, *id.,* at 9025–9026; Fulbright, *id.,* at 9599–9600; and Ellender, *id.,* at 9600.

the basis of race or color." 110 Cong. Rec. 7247.[11] (Emphasis added.) Despite these assurances, Senator Tower of Texas introduced an amendment authorizing "professionally developed ability tests." Proponents of Title VII opposed the amendment because, as written, it would permit an employer to give any test, "whether it was a good test or not, so long as it was professionally designed. Discrimination could actually exist under the guise of compliance with the statute." 110 Cong. Rec. 13504 (remarks of Sen. Case).

The amendment was defeated and two days later Senator Tower offered a substitute amendment which was adopted verbatim and is now the testing provision of § 703 (h). Speaking for the supporters of Title VII, Senator Humphrey, who had vigorously opposed the first amendment, endorsed the substitute amendment, stating: "Senators on both sides of the aisle who were deeply interested in title VII have examined the text of this amendment and have found it to be in accord with the intent and purpose of that title." 110 Cong. Rec. 13724. The amendment

11. The Court of Appeals majority, in finding no requirement in Title VII that employment tests be job related, relied in part on a quotation from an earlier Clark-Case interpretative memorandum addressed to the question of the constitutionality of Title VII. The Senators said in that memorandum:

"There is no requirement in title VII that employers abandon bona fide qualification tests where, because of differences in background and education, members of some groups are able to perform better on these tests than members of other groups. An employer may set his qualifications as high as he likes, he may test to determine which applicants have these qualifications, and he may hire, assign, and promote on the basis of test performance." 110 Cong. Rec. 7213.

However, nothing there stated conflicts with the later memorandum dealing specifically with the debate over employer testing, 110 Cong. Rec. 7247 (quoted from in the text above), in which Senators Clark and Case explained that tests which measure "applicable job qualifications" are permissible under Title VII. In the earlier memorandum Clark and Case assured the Senate that employers were not to be prohibited from using tests that determine *qualifications*. Certainly a reasonable interpretation of what the Senators meant, in light of the subsequent memorandum directed specifically at employer testing, was that nothing in the Act prevents employers from requiring that applicants be fit for the job.

was then adopted.[12] From the sum of the legislative history relevant in this case, the conclusion is inescapable that the EEOC's construction of § 703 (h) to require that employment tests be job related comports with congressional intent.

Nothing in the Act precludes the use of testing or measuring procedures; obviously they are useful. What Congress has forbidden is giving these devices and mechanisms controlling force unless they are demonstrably a reasonable measure of job performance. Congress has not commanded that the less qualified be preferred over the better qualified simply because of minority origins. Far from disparaging job qualifications as such, Congress has made such qualifications the controlling factor, so that race, religion, nationality, and sex become irrelevant. What Congress has commanded is that any tests used must measure the person for the job and not the person in the abstract.

The judgment of the Court of Appeals is, as to that portion of the judgment appealed from, reversed.

MR. JUSTICE BRENNAN took no part in the consideration or decision of this case.

12. Senator Tower's original amendment provided in part that a test would be permissible "if . . . in the case of any individual who is seeking employment with such employer, such test is designed to determine or predict whether such individual is suitable or trainable with respect to his employment in the particular business or enterprise involved. . . ." 110 Cong. Rec. 13492. This language indicates that Senator Tower's aim was simply to make certain that job-related tests would be permitted. The opposition to the amendment was based on its loose wording which the proponents of Title VII feared would be susceptible to misinterpretation. The final amendment, which was acceptable to all sides, could hardly have required less of a job relation than the first.

Documents

Remedy for Seniority-Based Advancement

United Steelworkers of America v. *Weber,* 443 U.S. 193
(1979) [Excerpt]

In 1974 the United Steelworkers of America and the Kaiser Aluminum and Chemical Corp. entered into a collective bargaining agreement. This agreement included an affirmative action plan designed to
eliminate conspicuous racial imbalances in Kaiser's almost all-white
craftwork force, by reserving 50 percent of the openings in plant
craft-training programs for black employees. During the plan's first
year of operation, seven black and six whites were selected from the
plant's production work force. The most senior black trainee had less
seniority than some white production workers who had been rejected
for the training program. Weber, a white production worker who had
been rejected for training, brought a class-action suit alleging that the
affirmative action plan was in violation of the Civil Rights Act of
1964. Although the District Court and the Court of Appeals supported that conclusion, this Supreme Court decision reversed it.

Challenged here is the legality of an affirmative action plan—
collectively bargained by an employer and a union—that reserves for black employees 50 percent of the openings in an in-
plant craft-training program until the percentage of black craftworkers in the plant is commensurate with the percentage of
blacks in the local labor force. The question for decision is
whether Congress, in Title VII of the Civil Rights Act of 1964, 78
Stat. 253, as amended, 42 U.S.C. (para.) 2000e *et seq.,* left
employers and unions in the private sector free to take such race-
conscious steps to eliminate manifest racial imbalances in traditionally segregated job categories. We hold that Title VII does not
prohibit such race-conscious affirmative action plans. . . .

. . . Given the legislative history, we cannot agree with respon-
dent that Congress intended to prohibit the private sector from
taking effective steps to accomplish the goal that Congress designed Title VII to achieve. The very statutory words intended as
a spur or catalyst to cause "employers and unions to self-examine

and to self-evaluate their employment practices and to endeavor to eliminate, so far as possible, the last vestiges of an unfortunate and ignominious page in this country's history," . . . cannot be interpreted as an absolute prohibition against all private, voluntary, race-conscious affirmative action efforts to hasten the elimination of such vestiges. It would be ironic indeed if a law triggered by a Nation's concern over centuries of racial injustice and intended to improve the lot of those who had "been excluded from the American dream for so long," 110 Cong. Rec. 6552 (1964) (remarks of Sen. Humphrey), constituted the first legislative prohibition of all voluntary, private, race-conscious efforts to abolish traditional patterns of racial segregation and hierarchy. . . .

We need not today define in detail the line of demarcation between permissible and impermissible affirmative action plans. It suffices to hold that the challenged Kaiser-USWA affirmative action plan falls on the permissible side of the line. The purposes of the plan mirror those of the statute. Both were designed to break down old patterns of racial segregation and hierarchy. Both were structured to "open employment opportunities for Negroes in occupations which have been traditionally closed to them." 110 Cong. Rec. 6548 (1964) (remarks of Sen. Humphrey).

At the same time, the plan does not unnecessarily trammel the interests of the white employees. The plan does not require the discharge of white workers and their replacement with new black hires. . . . Nor does the plan create an absolute bar to the advancement of white employees; half of those trained in the program will be white. Moreover, the plan is a temporary measure; it is not intended to maintain racial balance, but simply to eliminate a manifest racial imbalance. Preferential selection of craft trainees at the Gramercy plant will end as soon as the percentage of black skilled craftworkers in the Gramercy plant approximates the percentage of blacks in the local labor force.

Remedies for Seniority-Based Layoff

Work-sharing: Eleanor Holmes Norton, "Layoffs and Equal Employment Opportunity," *Federal Register* 45 (September 12, 1980) [Excerpt]

Congress enacted Title VII to improve the economic and social conditions for minorities and women by providing equal opportunities in the workplace. As a result of this legislation, in the late 1960's and early 1970's, many new employment opportunities opened up to minorities and women in areas where they had been previously denied access.

As many minorities and women have only recently been hired, many of them have not yet had time to accrue seniority sufficient to withstand layoffs. In recessionary periods, such as the current one, they are therefore usually the first to be laid off when an employer finds it necessary to reduce its labor needs. The Commission is greatly concerned that because such layoffs usually have an adverse impact on minorities and women, the routine use of layoffs on a last-hired, first-fired basis, is beginning to eradicate many recent affirmative gains made in the workplace. The Commission is, therefore, interested in investigating alternative approaches to layoffs which would satisfy the employer's reduced labor needs with a minimum of adverse impact on minorities and women. In this regard, the Commission is seeking information from the widest range of people and organizations who are affected by layoffs.

•

In *Griggs* v. *Duke Power Co.*, 401 U.S. 424 (1971), the Supreme Court held that neutral employment practices are discriminatory where they have an adverse impact on minorities and women and cannot be justified by business necessity. The Court of Appeals in

Remedies: Recommendation for Work-Sharing

Robinson v. *Lorillard,* 444 F. 2d 791 (4th Cir. 1971), held that in order to establish a business necessity for using an employment practice which has such an adverse impact, the employer must demonstrate that there are no available alternatives which would accomplish the employer's business purposes with a lesser adverse impact on minorities or women.

· · · ·

There are very substantial incentives which should prompt employers to consider alternatives to layoffs. For example, as noted above, by not routinely resorting to layoffs, an employer may be able to avoid potential liability under Title VII as well as Executive Order 11246. Additionally, as the economy has become increasingly dependent on technology, the cost of training new employees has become a much greater part of the employers' investment, as compared to prior periods when the economy was dominated by unskilled and semi-skilled manufacturing jobs and workers. When an employer lays off a worker today the employer often loses the considerable investment that an experienced and trained workforce represents. Therefore, in today's economy, it is to the employer's advantage to explore alternative means of reducing labor costs which to the greatest extent possible avoid laying off workers.

There are substantial incentives for labor organizations too. Some alternative approaches would result in most workers, not only the minorities and female workers, keeping their jobs, and thus affording protection against layoffs to all union members generally. For example, if worksharing were the selected alternative, greater job security would also be afforded to the less senior white workers who might otherwise be subject to being laid off. Furthermore, any approach that would keep most of its members employed, would also provide the union with the strength that an active dues paying membership provides.

•

Signed at Washington D.C., this 9th day of September 1980
For the Commission.

Eleanor Holmes Norton
Chair, Equal Employment Opportunity Commission

Racial Preference: *Vulcan Pioneers* v. *New Jersey
Department of Civil Service,* 34 Fair Empl. Prac. Cas.
(BNA) 1239 (D.N.J. 1984) [Excerpt]

This matter arose out of a suit filed in 1977 by the United States
charging the New Jersey Department of Civil Service with discrimi-
nating against minorities. In 1980 a consent decree (a court-ordered
agreement) led to an increase in the proportion of minority firefighters. In 1983 after the City of Newark announced that it would be
laying off 76 firefighters, 46 of whom were minorities, Vulcan Pioneers, an organization of black and hispanic firefighters from Newark, attempted to restrain the minority layoff. This court ordered that
layoffs should be undertaken in a manner that did not undermine the
purpose of the affirmative action plan. This decision, however, was
effectively invalidated later in the same year by *Firefighters Local
Union No. 1784* v. *Stotts* (1984); hence the court order based on this
decision was withdrawn.

SAROKIN, District Judge:—This matter presents to the court
one of the most difficult and troubling issues facing the judiciary
today. Either by court order or consent decree, minorities have
been hired as police officers and firefighters in major cities
throughout the country. The clear purpose of such orders was
and is to affirmatively correct the imbalances which have resulted
from a history of discriminatory practices in the hiring and promotion of minorities.

Many of these orders, including the one here at issue, do not
provide for specific procedures to be followed in the event of
layoffs. If the dictates of seniority are to govern, then minorities,
being the most recently hired, will be laid off and the goals of
affirmative action undermined. If, on the other hand, an attempt

is made to protect such minority hires, then persons with greater seniority will be compelled to forfeit positions guaranteed by contract and statute. It is the tension between these two alternatives which renders the resolution of this problem so difficult.

The court, however, is convinced that adherence to strict contractual and statutory seniority requirements in determining who shall go and who shall stay cannot be permitted. The affirmative action plan embodied in the consent decree between the parties and the hirings pursuant thereto would be substantially eradicated thereby. The gains contemplated and those achieved would be lost. Furthermore, a municipality or the state would be able to avoid the effect of such an order or decree merely by withholding the funds necessary to effectuate it. This type of unilateral action should not be permitted to thwart a judicial order or to justify the breach of a consent decree.

Affirmative action plans arose out of the recognition that this nation had oppressed its minority citizens, either purposefully or through the operation of more subtle social and economic forces. These plans seek more than to remove the nation's heel from the backs of minorities, but to reach down and to lift up those persons who have been deprived and discriminated against for centuries. The plans recognize the insufficiency of merely removing existing barriers. Affirmative action is necessary in order that historical imbalances and inequities not be prolonged well into the future.

Having recognized that obligation and acted upon it, are we to undo it in the face of economic reductions? Indeed, in hard economic times, it has always been the minorities who have suffered the most. It would be a dreadful step backwards to permit mass layoffs of minorities in light of the progress so recently achieved and so long in coming.

Changes in administration, changes in the composition of the Civil Rights Commission, indeed, changes in the government's position in this very litigation, should not alter the fundamental principles here involved. We cannot and should not retreat from

our commitment to right the wrongs of the past. To permit layoffs based solely on seniority denies these principles and mocks
the ideals of justice and equality which are the foundation of our
Constitution and of the Civil Rights Act.

By virtue of this determination, certain firefighters and police
officers with greater seniority will be required to forfeit their positions. Were it not for the consent decree, these firefighters and
police officers would be entitled to retain their positions under existing collective bargaining agreements and New Jersey civil service law. Though not themselves the perpetrators of the wrongs
inflicted upon minorities over the years, these senior firefighters
are being singled out to suffer the consequences. In effect, they are
being required to hand over their jobs and paychecks to someone
else. It is inconceivable that they can be asked to do this in the
name of the public good, and yet not have the public assume the
responsibility therefor. If we need to raze buildings to make way
for a highway, to acquire land for a school or to obtain food to
feed the poor, we do not simply take it from those who have it.
What is involved in such cases is a taking of private property, and
the Constitution requires that just compensation be paid.

Such a taking also occurs when the federal government, pursuant to civil rights legislation brings a lawsuit to enforce those
laws and enters into a consent decree which adversely affects the
contractual and statutory rights of private individuals. In such a
situation, it is the federal government which must assume the
resulting liability. It would be senseless to impose such liability
upon the municipalities involved. Layoffs made in good faith, for
economic reasons, may not be prohibited, for to do so would
deny cities the right to reduce expenses. Moreover, if these municipalities could afford to pay just compensation, then they
could afford to retain the workers. Requiring cities to pay persons whom they laid off because they could not afford to keep
them would be ludicrous.

The court is therefore satisfied that the federal government must compensate senior firefighters laid off as a result of the application of the consent decree. The compensation to be paid is outlined below. However, the court recognizes that such compensation is small consolation to those who will nonetheless lose their jobs. Displaced senior firefighters and their families may well ask, "Why us?"

No truly satisfactory answer exists. Their perception of the unfairness visited upon them cannot be dissipated by a discussion of principle or of broad social goals. They cannot be expected to understand why they should pay for what others have wrought or why they should be singled out and forced to make an involuntary contribution to a cause not their own, no matter how worthy that cause may be.

If the analogy to taking for highway purposes is apt, then those whose homes are taken probably pose the same question. Compensation is not adequate reparation for the personal displacement and upset, and the need for a public corridor does not allay their personal loss. Affirmative action is also a highway of sorts. It provides an avenue of hope, a road to equality. However, to ignore the grief and anger of those who fall in its path is to be blind to a poignant reality of our times. One can only hope that those called upon to make a sacrifice will not permit it to escalate the prejudice which it seeks to undo. They must recognize that affirmative action is likewise small compensation for those who are descendants of slavery and have continued to be victims of insidious bondage for generations since its abolition.

·

[I]t is the intention of the court that, in the event of layoffs, the same proportion of minorities survive reductions in force as were employed prior to such reductions. Only to the extent the hiring goals were actually achieved shall they therefore be maintained. Those who are kept and those who are not will be determined in accordance with seniority to the maximum extent possible. It is only if this results in a disproportionate effect upon minority employees that an adjustment need be made, and such adjustment should itself reflect employees' respective seniority positions. Thus, as between two nonminority employees, one of whom must be laid off in order to maintain the proper proportion of minority firefighters, the least senior must go. Furthermore, the system here put in place by the court is, of course, meant to be temporary. When, in the course of time, minority firefighters attain the seniority rightfully theirs, this kind of relief will no longer be necessary, for they will then be laid off, in the event of economic hardship, in the proper proportions. In the meantime, however, a system is necessary that will protect the affirmative action plan now in place and just beginning to have its effect.

·

The court also concludes that those firefighters who have or will forfeit their seniority rights as a result of the affirmative action plan discussed above ought to be compensated and that such compensation ought to come from the federal government.

·

The amount of such compensation must, however, be "just." It is not intended to be a lifetime pension. Those senior firefighters who are laid off as a result of an affirmative action plan shall be under a duty to mitigate damages, by seeking to obtain other employment. Any claim for compensation shall be reduced by the amount of salaries or any benefits received as a result of such layoffs. Moreover, the period of compensation shall end upon the attainment of other employment, but, absent exceptional circumstances, no later than one year from the date of layoff.

•

This country owes a debt to its minority citizens to compensate them for generations of degradation and deprivation. The debt is being partially repaid by providing opportunities heretofore denied. To withdraw those opportunities now constitutes a denial of our democratic principles and a breach of faith to those who have fought and even died for them and to whom we promised that tomorrow would be better.

7

A Response to Moral Critics
of Affirmative Action

Opinion of Justice Thurgood Marshall: *Regents of
University of California* v. *Bakke,* 438 U.S. 265 (1978)
(Marshall, J., concurring in part and dissenting in part
[Excerpt]

The medical school of the University of California at Davis had both a
general admission program and a special program for minority and
economically or educationally disadvantaged applicants. Allan Bakke
was rejected in 1973 and 1974 under the general admission program.
In both years special program applicants were admitted with significantly lower scores than Bakke's. He filed a suit in a California state
court alleging that the special admission program was in violation of
the Civil Rights Act of 1964 and the U.S. Constitution. The U.S.
Supreme Court affirmed that the special admission program was
invalid but that in future admissions decisions race could be taken
into account. In this opinion, Justice Marshall stated that he agreed
with the decision only insofar as it permits a university to consider an
applicant's race in making an admission decision.

It is unnecessary in 20th century America to have individual
Negroes demonstrate that they have been victims of racial dis-

crimination; the racism of our society has been so pervasive that none, regardless of wealth or position, has managed to escape its impact. The experience of Negroes in America has been different in kind, not just in degree, from that of other ethnic groups. It is not merely the history of slavery alone but also that a whole people were marked as inferior by the law. And that mark has endured. The dream of America as the great melting pot has not been realized for the Negro; because of his skin color he never even made it into the pot. . . .

It is because of a legacy of unequal treatment that we now must permit the institutions of this society to give consideration to race in making decisions about who will hold the positions of influence, affluence and prestige in America. For far too long the doors to those positions have been shut to Negroes. If we are ever to become a fully integrated society, one in which the color of a person's skin will not determine the opportunities available to him or her, we must be willing to take steps to open those doors. I do not believe that anyone can truly look into America's past and still find that a remedy for the effects of that past is impermissible.

Index

Index

Index

textile industry and, 48
"Unique Competence, A": A Study of Equal Employment Opportunity in the Bell System, 97–108
voluntary affirmative action guidelines, 41–42
work-sharing and, 44, 125
Equal Protection Clause (Fourteenth Amendment), 109
European immigrants, 57–58
Executive Order 11246, 37, 49, 68–70, 125
Expansion Proposal, 66–67

Federal Housing Authority (FHA), racist policies of, 74–75
Firefighters Local Union No. 1784 v. Stotts et al., 45, 50, 126
Fischer, John H., 21
Fleming, Harold C., 34
Foner, Nancy, 60
Fourteenth Amendment, Equal Protection Clause of, 109
Franklin, John Hope, 21
Fullilove v. Klutznick, 37

Gaston County v. United States, 116
General Electric, 43
German immigrants, 58
Gewin, Walter P., 108
Glazer, Nathan, 55–57
Glickstein, Howard, 43, 45–46
Goldman, Alan, 90, 92–93
Good faith versus numerical goals, 33–38
Goudia, Kernell, 19–20
Gould, William B., 36
Greek immigrants, 58
Griggs v. Duke Power Co., 39–40, 50, 69, 70, 88–89, 111–21, 124

Harvard Law Review, 24
Harvard University, 22
Hiring. *See* Numerical goals; Preferential treatment
Humphrey, Hubert H., 120, 123

IBM, 48
Illinois Bell, 100
Institutional racism, 26–27
Bell System example, 84, 97–108
overt racism compared to, 9–11
personal connections and, 14–18
qualification requirements and, 18–23
seniority and, 24–26
International Ladies' Garment Workers Union, 58
Irish immigrants, 58
Ironworkers' Union, 15, 23
Italian immigrants, 58

Jackson, Don, 78–79
Jencks, Christopher, 61
Jewish immigrants, 57–58
Joint Center for Political Studies, 13

Kaiser Aluminum and Chemical Company, 19–20, 35, 46, 122–23
Korean immigrants, 59

Labor unions:
affirmative action and, 31, 35–36
Firefighters Local Union No. 1784 v. Stotts et al., 45, 50, 126
racism and anti-union efforts, 84
successes of other (nonblack) minorities and, 58
United Steelworkers of America v. Weber, 19–20, 46, 70, 71, 122–23

Index

Index

Index

Library of Congress Cataloging-in-Publication Data

Ezorsky, Gertrude, 1926–
    Racism and justice : the case for affirmative action / Gertrude Ezorsky.
        p.   cm.
    Includes index.
    ISBN 0-8014-2622-7 (alk. paper). — ISBN 0-8014-9922-4 (pbk. : alk. paper)
    1. Affirmative action programs—United States. 2. Discrimination in employment—United States. 3. Race discrimination—United States. I. Title.
HF5549.5.A34E97 1991
331.13′3′0973—dc20   91-55062